商务英语口语实战丛书

国际商务英语口语

Spoken English for International Business

（修订本）

中级

主　编　张礼贵　廖国强　刘春智
副主编　蒋华应　黄　强　杨德洪

清华大学出版社
北京交通大学出版社
·北京·

内 容 简 介

本书共9个单元，主要内容包括商务会展，询盘、报盘与还盘，接受或成交，资信调查，订购与确认，支付，商务物流，商业保险，对产品与服务的投诉及受理等涉外商务活动。

本书适用于高等院校商务英语及相关专业的学生，同时也适用于国际商务活动的从业者和爱好者。

图书在版编目（CIP）数据

国际商务英语口语：中级／张礼贵，廖国强，刘春智主编. — 修订本. — 北京：北京交通大学出版社：清华大学出版社，2019.1（2024.10修订）

ISBN 978-7-5121-1798-3

Ⅰ. ①国…　Ⅱ. ①张…　②廖…　③刘…　Ⅲ. ①国际商务-英语-口语　Ⅳ. ①H319.9

中国版本图书馆 CIP 数据核字（2014）第 018721 号

国际商务英语口语（中级）

GUOJI SHANGWU YINGYU KOUYU（ZHONGJI）

责任编辑：张利军

出版发行：清华大学出版社　　邮编：100084　　电话：010-62776969　http://www.tup.com.cn

北京交通大学出版社　　邮编：100044　　电话：010-51686414　http://www.bjtup.com.cn

印　刷　者：北京鑫海金澳胶印有限公司

经　　销：全国新华书店

开　　本：185 mm×243 mm　　印张：10.5　　字数：308 千字

版 印 次：2024 年 10 月第 1 版第 1 次修订　2024 年 10 月第 4 次印刷

定　　价：39.00元

本书如有质量问题，请向北京交通大学出版社质监组反映。对您的意见和批评，我们表示欢迎和感谢。

投诉电话：010-51686043，51686008；传真：010-62225406；E-mail：press@bjtu.edu.cn。

加入世界贸易组织，标志着我国对外开放新的全方位的推进。在经济全球化的新形势下，中国与世界各国的商务交流与合作也会更加频繁。作为一门通用的国际性语言，英语在国际商务交流中起着极其重要的作用。从事涉外商务工作的人员需要掌握好英语，特别是英语口语，才能更好地开展商务活动。

《国际商务英语口语》正是基于这样的背景而为从事对外经贸工作和其他涉外工作的人员及相关学习者编写的商务英语口语读本，既可以作为高等院校商务英语及相关专业学生的口语教材，又可以作为一种工具书，供相关的学习者参考模仿之用。

《国际商务英语口语》共 3 册，分为初级、中级和高级，主要内容涵盖了对外商务往来中最为常见的经典对话场景，基本上由易到难渐进地涉及了涉外贸易中所有主要的商务活动。

《国际商务英语口语》在选材上覆盖面广，代表性和针对性强，并且兼具实用性和生动性。在实用性方面，书中所选取的材料均为商务活动中最常见的场景，具有很强的实践性和可操作性，能够有效地帮助学习者进行针对性极强的训练并学以致用，符合应用型人才培养的要求。在生动性方面，书中所选取的材料具有较强的趣味性，易学易懂，能够充分地调动起不同层次学习者的学习兴趣。

《国际商务英语口语》在体系的编排上科学合理。

每单元的开始部分均提供了与本单元话题相关的文化背景，以帮助学习者对此话题有一个更加准确的把握。每单元的主体是日常商务对话的经典范例及常用词汇、句型，学习者可以此为模板学习并熟练掌握其中的一些对话技巧。每单元还就对话中出现的语言难点及重要的国际商务知识给出了详尽的注释，以帮助学习者更深入地理解本单元的主题。每单元的课后练习也紧紧围绕本单元的话题展开，主要有"根据中文提示补全对话"和"根据提供的对话背景模仿特定人物进行情景对话"两大类实操性训练。

为了让学习者能够在涉外商务活动中有效地进行交流，每单元后还附有本单元对话的译文，以供学习者参阅。为了让学习者能够更好地掌握相关话题的对话技巧，每单元最后均提供了与之相关的扩展阅读材料，并留有让学习者参与讨论的问题。

本书为《国际商务英语口语》的中级本，共9个单元，主要涵盖商务会展，询盘、报盘与还盘，接受或成交，资信调查，订购与确认，支付，商务物流，商业保险，对产品与服务的投诉及受理等涉外贸易中常见的商务活动。

本书以二维码的形式动态地向读者提供相关的教学资源，读者可先扫描封底上的防盗码获得资源读取权限，然后再根据自身的学习需求，通过扫描每单元开始处的二维码，获取并使用相关的教学资源。例如，本书中所有的对话均配有地道的 MP3 录音，学习者扫描二维码后即可收听，并可对照本书的教学材料进行对话模仿训练。

本书在编写过程中参考了大量的文献资料，在此向这些文献资料的作者表示衷心的感谢。编者也殷切地希望本书能够对相关读者的商务英语学习有所帮助。然而，鉴于编者水平有限，书中难免有错漏之处，恳请广大读者批评指正。

编者
2024 年 10 月

目 录

CONTENTS

Unit

1

Business Convention and Exhibition

商 务 会 展

Learning Resources

Warming-up

A business convention and exhibition is an exhibition or a business gathering organized by companies that show their new products and services and also their latest offerings. Business conventions and exhibitions provide opportunities for companies to meet their customers, to compare their products with those of their competitors, to learn new trends and to identify new prospects. They also provide opportunities for customers to have the ability to closely examine competitive products.

Business conventions and exhibitions are not open to the public but can only be attended by company representatives, members of the trade and members of the press. One advantage of a business convention and exhibition is that it shortens the time it takes for companies to look for prospective customers while the major disadvantage is that customers usually cannot concentrate on many exhibitors and their products due to the distractions and the busy atmosphere.

In a business convention and exhibition they often use devices for displays including banner stands, booths and counters, panel display, etc. The business convention and exhibition booth is an important component of the trade show display as it aims to enhance the brand and facilitates valuable for face-to-face contact between the companies and their prospective customers. All the above devices clearly display the company logo and give customers a better understanding of the products or services being marketed.

Dialogues

▶ **Dialogue 1** **Preparing for a Trade Show**

Ms. Black (B), sales manager of a pharmaceutical plant, is going to publicize her product in a mini trade show. She is now talking the matter over with Mr. Li (L), manager of Liaotong Advertisement Co., Ltd.

B: First, allow me to give you a brief introduction of our company. We are a joint venture with Canada and one of the largest manufactures of medicine in Northeast China. In order to push sales of one of our new products into the market, our company is thinking of attending the mini trade show held next month in this city. I wonder if you are interested in helping us in this respect.

L: It would be a great pleasure to us. But, first of all, could you tell me what you want so that I can see where I could be of help.

B: First, we'd like to ask you to help with balloons with slogans on them, and working staff, etc.

L: No problem. We do have such facilities, and we have etiquette ladies to help with the reception etiquette and some guides to help and propagate your product.

B: That's fine. In order to make our show well-known to people, I have prepared some straightforward literature in both Chinese and English. I wonder if you can help us to have it designed more impressively and attractively.

L: Small case, it's our job. We'll surely do well. We suggest you to put an ad in the local newspaper as well as posts on the bulletins to make the coming show widely known to the public.

B: Good suggestion. By the way, we're going to invite some famous doctors from the local hospitals to help us offer free medical diagnosis and advice to the public. So could you please make a list of the doctors possibly invited?

L: That sound like s a good idea. I'll think about it and contact them.

▶ Dialogue 2   At a Chinese Ceramics Exhibit

In the exhibition hall, a Chinese ceramist (C) is talking with an American (A).

A: What beautiful art ceramics you make!

C: I learned the craft from my father. Then I studied ceramic engineering at school.

A: All your hard work looks as if it's paid off.

C: Yes, I have 50 employees. I hope to become the biggest exporter of ceramics in China.

A: Well, the demand for ceramics is increasing in my country.

C: Yes, a large proportion of our sales are to the US.

A: The development of ceramics in your country has been remarkable. You carry on a centuries-old tradition and keep pace with modern technology at the same time.

C: Yes, our research in the field has been yielding good results. And we are deeply grateful to

3

your country's technicians for their considerable assistance.

A: Would you please tell me about your designs?

C: How do you like this one?

A: It's beautiful.

C: This is an eight-foot decorative vase. It's hand-made and the inland designs are etched in. It takes 45 days to make. Its retail price will be US$3,000.

A: The result is certainly worth the effort. How about this design over there?

C: This vase is still in the experimental stage.

A: Why is that?

C: It's quite expensive to make and because of its small size, buyers balk at its high price. We feel we could sell more if we could reduce the price.

A: Well, you mustn't tamper with quality. It's the high quality of Chinese ceramics that attracts American buyers.

C: That's why a reduction in price can never be made at the expense of quality.

A: Well, thank you for showing me your beautiful ceramic ware. I was so impressed by your designs and the high quality of your pieces.

▶ **Dialogue 3**　**On the Way to an Electronic Exhibition**

Miss Lin (L) is waiting for her flight to Chicago in the departure lounge when she notices a man (B) next to her reading an electronic magazine. She comes to the man and starts a talk with him.

L: Excuse me. I notice you are reading an electronic magazine. Do you know there is a big electronic exhibition in Chicago starting tomorrow?

B: Of course! That's the reason I'm going to Chicago. Hi! My name is Barney Miller. What's your name, please?

L: Junior Lin. I'm sales representative for Woofers Inc., based in China. Are you looking forward to the exhibition?

B: Huh, I've been waiting to go to this show for more than three months. There are going to be companies from over forty different countries there.

L: I know. I'm really looking forward to seeing what new products will be on the market next year.

B: I'm more interested in the new discoveries which are being made in the electronics industry.

L: Really? Do you mind if I ask what part of the electronics industry you are in?

B: Not at all. I work in the R&D department of a company based in Los-Angeles. We specialize in designing printers.

L: What's the name of your company? Maybe I've heard of it.

B: I don't think so. We're just a little company called "Halcyon".

L: Hmm. Oh, didn't you come out with an amazingly small but strong high-tech printer at the exhibition last year in New York?

B: Yeah, that turned out to be our best seller of the year, but every one forgets our name.

L: One of my jobs is to look for the products that will be the most successful, and then find out why. So I don't just remember the big companies.

B: I like the way you think. Would you like to get together for dinner when we arrive in Chicago, so we can talk more about this?

▶ **Dialogue 4** **Ordering a Booth**

Rachel (R) comes to the exhibition center to order a booth. Phillip (P), the receptionist of the center, is serving her.

R: Good morning, sir. I'd like to reserve a booth for our company. This is my card. How many spots are there left?

P: I still have several prime spots in high-traffic areas. But they are going fast. *(Shows a floor plan)* How about this corner booth? It's close to the main entrance.

R: Pricey, I'm sure. We just need to be close to our major competitors. Where are they?

P: Some haven't confirmed yet, but they are mostly in this area.

R: Booth C322 looks like a good spot.

P: It's close to the restrooms. Lots of traffic. A deal at two thousand dollars.

R: That's steep. We paid about half that last year.

P: But we're going with a flat fee this year to make everyone's life easier. And we are also expecting a fifteen percent increase in attendance.

R: So, commissions and entrance fee distributions are no longer part of the package?

P: That's right. And we've stepped up our marketing plan. Did you notice the advertising in the *Times*?

R: Yes, I did see that. What about credit card payment machines and Internet hookup?

P: The same as last year, an additional fifty dollars.

R: All right. We'll go with booth C322.

Words and Expressions

gathering   *n.* 集会，聚会

offering   *n.* 奉献，提供，待售物

identify   *v.* 识别，确定

prospect   *n.* 前景，可能性，机会，可能成为主顾的人

member of the trade   行业会员

the press   新闻界

prospective   *a.* 预期的，未来的，即将发生的

distraction   *n.* 分散注意力（或分心）的事物

device   *n.* 手段，手法，技巧，设备

banner stand   易拉宝

booth   *n.* （隔开的）小房间，封闭的隔间，展示间，货摊，展位

panel   *n.* 镶板，嵌板，护墙板

component   *n.* 组成部分

enhance   *v.* 提高，增强

facilitate   *v.* 使更容易，便于，促进

logo   *n.* 标识，商标

propagate   *v.* 传播，宣传

floor plan   会场平面图

hookup   *n.* 连接线路

Notes

1. 参加商务会展的有关注意事项如下。

（1）多渠道选展。要尽可能多地了解展览会资料，这是做出正确决策的有效保证。有关展览会的资料可向各主办机构索取，行业杂志和互联网上也会有详细的介绍。

（2）提前一年做好参展计划。德国商家的计划性是世界闻名的，一位德国展览公司的负责人建议：一切计划要在一年前做好。他认为，中国参展团一般计划做得较迟，再加上其他种种原因，参展消息到达对方时，已经太晚。

（3）展品要适宜可销。据科隆家电展览中心的统计，到德国参展的客商中有72%是为了寻求新产品，所以不要展示过时产品。为了确保产品"适宜可销"，参展前的市场调查非常重要。

（4）要把资料准备充分。据悉，中国赴外参展的企业中，普遍存在资料准备不充分

的问题。一些厂家甚至对产品的介绍只有三言两语，并且不配外文翻译，往往把整理资料的工作推给组织方，这样一来不仅耽误了时间，而且临时的翻译有时很难完全表达厂家的意图。

（5）目标客户要事先约定。可向公司现有客户邮寄邀请信或通过 E-mail 通知。同重要的客户约定见面时间，以加强业务联系。一位经常出展的专业人士建议，中国出口商应在展前有意识地邀请目标客户参观自己的展位，从而避免展览会上自己的展台门庭冷落的情况发生，力争给目标买家留下深刻的印象。

2. a joint venture with Canada   与加拿大合营的合资企业

3. push sales   推销

4. in this respect   在这个方面

5. balloons with slogans on   写有宣传标语的气球

6. working staff   工作人员

7. etiquette lady   礼仪小姐

8. reception etiquette   迎送礼仪

9. straightforward literature   明确易懂的说明书

10. Small case, it's our job.   小事一桩，这是我们的工作。

11. offer free medical diagnosis and advice to the public   提供义诊和免费咨询

12. Its retail price will be US$3,000.   零售价是 3 000 美元。

13. This vase is still in the experimental stage.   这个花瓶还在实验阶段。

14. We feel we could sell more if we could reduce the price.
    我们认为，如果售价降低，将能卖出更多。

15. That's why a reduction in price can never be made at the expense of quality.
    那就是为什么降低价格的同时不能以牺牲质量为代价。

16. that turned out to be our best seller of the year   成为年度最畅销产品。

Useful Sentences

● 准备参加商展常用句型

1. I think it would greatly benefit our company to attend the trade show at…
   我认为在……参展，公司会大大受益。

2. All of our competition will be exhibiting, so…
   我们的竞争对手都会参展，所以……

3. I think our booth needs information brochures…
  我认为我们的摊位需要有关产品的资讯手册……

4. If you come to our booth at trade show, I can demonstrate our…
  如果你能在商展时光顾我们的摊位，我会示范我们的……

5. This product is the result of our latest technology.
  这一产品是我们最新的技术成果。

6. Two of the most popular trade shows are held in Beijing and Shanghai.
  两个最热门的商展是在北京和上海举办的。

7. Many of our competitors will be participating at the Hong Kong Export Trade Show.
  我们有许多的竞争对手将会参加香港出口贸易展览会。

8. Please take this information for your reference.
  这些资料送给你做参考。

9. There is a great demand for this new product.
  这种新产品的需求量很大。

10. Let me show you how to operate this machine.
  让我来为你示范如何操作这部机器。

11. Here is all the information you need.
  你需要的信息都在这里。

12. We can just take a glance at the exhibition.
  我们只需稍稍浏览一下这个展会。

13. We're like to order your products.
  我们想订你们的货。

14. This is my first to the Fair.
  这是我首次参加交易会。

15. I was wondering if you had the time to show me around this exhibition.
  不知你是否有时间带我参观一下这个展览会。

16. I found some of the exhibits fine in quality and beautiful in design.
  我发现一些展品的质量不错，而且设计也很漂亮。

- **会展常用句型**

1. Let me introduce you to Mr. Li, general manager of our company.
  让我介绍你认识一下李先生，他是我们公司的总经理。

2. It's an honor to meet you.
  很荣幸认识你。

3. Nice to meet you. I've heard a lot about you.
很高兴认识你，久仰大名。

4. How do I pronounce your name?
你的名字怎么读？

5. How do I address you?
如何称呼您？

6. It's going to be the pride of our company.
这将是本公司的荣幸。

7. What line of business are you in?
你是做哪一行的？

8. Keep in touch.
保持联系。

9. Thank you for coming.
谢谢你的光临。

10. Don't mention it.
别客气

11. Excuse me for interrupting you.
请原谅我打扰你。

12. I'm sorry to disturb you.
对不起，打扰你一下。

13. Excuse me a moment.
对不起，失陪一下。

14. Excuse me. I'll be right back.
对不起，我马上回来。

15. What about the price?
你对价格有何看法？

16. What do you think of the payment terms?
你对支付条件有何看法？

17. How do you feel like the quality of our products?
你觉得我们产品的质量怎么样？

18. What about having a look at sample first?
先看一看样品如何？

19. What about placing a trial order?
何不先试订货？

20. The quality of ours is as good as that of many other suppliers, while our prices are not

so high as theirs. By the way, which items are you interested in?

我们的产品质量与其他供应商一样的好，而我们的价格却不像他们的那样高。顺便问一下，你对哪个产品感兴趣？

21. You can rest assured.

    你可以放心。

22. We are always improving our design and patterns to confirm to the world market.

    我们一直在提高我们产品的设计水平，以满足世界市场的要求。

23. This new product is to the taste of European market.

    这种新产品在欧洲市场很受欢迎。

24. I think it will also find a good market in your market.

    我认为它也会在贵国市场上畅销。

25. Fine quality as well as low price will help push the sales of your products.

    上乘的质量和较低的价格将有助于推动贵方产品的销售。

26. While we appreciate your cooperation, we regret to say that we can't reduce our price any further.

    虽然我们感谢贵方的合作，但是很抱歉，我们不能再减价了。

27. Reliability is our strong point.

    可靠性正是我们产品的优点。

28. We are satisfied with the quality of your samples, so the business depends entirely on your price.

    我们对样品的质量很满意，因此交易的成败就完全取决于你们的价格了。

29. To a certain extent, our price depends on how large your order is.

    在某种程度上，我们的价格取决于你们订单的大小。

30. This product is now in great demand and we have on hand many enquiries from other countries.

    这种产品现在需求量很大，我们手头上有来自其他国家的很多询盘。

31. Thank you for your inquiry. Would you tell us what quantity you require so that we can work out the offer?

    谢谢你询价。为了便于我方提出报价，能否请你告知你方需求的数量？

32. Here are our FOB price list. All the prices in the list are subject to our final confirmation.

    这是我们的 FOB 价格单。单上所有价格以我方最后确认为准。

33. In general, our prices are given on a FOB basis.

    通常我们的报价都是 FOB 价。

34. Our prices compare most favorably with quotations you can get from other manufacturers. You'll see that from our price sheet. The prices are subject to our confirmation,

naturally.

我们的价格比其他制造商优惠得多。这一点你可以从我们的价格单上看到。当然啦，所有价格要以我方最后确认为准。

35. We offer you our best prices, at which we have done a lot business with other customers.

我们向你们报最优惠价，按此价我们已与其他客户做了大批生意。

36. Will you please tell us the specifications, quantity and packing you want, so that we can work out the offer ASAP?

能否告诉我们贵方对规格、数量及包装的要求，以便我方尽快制订出报价？

37. This is the pricelist, but it serves as a guide line only. Is there anything you are particularly interested in?

这是价格表，但仅供参考。上面是否有你特别感兴趣的商品？

38. Do you have specific request for packing? Here are the samples of packing available now, and you may have a look.

你们对包装有什么特别要求吗？这是我们目前用的包装样品，你可以看一下。

39. I wonder if you have found that our specifications meet your requirements. I'm sure the prices we submitted are competitive.

我想知道您是否认为我们的规格符合您的要求。我敢肯定我们的价格是非常有竞争力的。

40. Heavy enquiries witness the quality of our products.

大量询盘证明我们的产品质量过硬。

41. We regret that the goods you inquire about are not available.

很遗憾，你们所询货物目前无货。

42. My offer was based on reasonable profit, not on wild speculations.

我的报价以合理利润为依据，不是漫天要价。

43. Moreover, we've kept the price close to the costs of production.

再说，我们的价格已经很接近成本价了。

44. Could you tell me which kind of payment terms you'll choose?

能否告知你们将采用哪种付款方式？

45. Would you accept delivery spread over a period of time?

你们能否接受在一段时间内分批交货？

Exercises

I Complete the following dialogues.

1. **A:** What should I do with the display items?

   B: You can sell some of the display items. For those that you cannot sell here, _____

   _____

   （另外再找一家运输公司，将不能出售的部分运回中国）.

2. **A:** Thank you. Without your help, _____

   （我不可能在展会上遇到这么多大客户）.

   B: You are welcome.

3. **A:** _____.

   （我们和两个新客户建立了贸易关系，签了总量为 2 000 万元人民币的丝绸裙子的订单。）

   B: You have done a good job!

4. **A:** Do you like the products we sold you?

   B: Yes. The cotton cheongsams are selling well, _____

   _____

   （尤其是那些具有中国传统图案和文字的式样更受欢迎）.

5. **A:** I like this booth very much and I plan to take part in the exhibition next year, too.

   B: _____.

   （我们会提前通知你明年的展览情况，并为你预留这个摊位。）

II Situational practice.

Make dialogues according to the following situations.

1. At the North Spring Trade Show, a Philippine dealer of electronic products, Winnie Cruz, is inquiring prices at the stand of a Chinese company. Now it's your turn to act as Winnie Cruz, and your partner as Miss Fengjuan, sales representative of the Chinese company.

2. Suppose you are Mr. Johnson, the sales representative of the American company. You arrive at the exhibition center but you find that your exhibits have not been there yet. You come to the service desk and ask the reason. Your partner acts as the service receptionist, Miss Windy.

对话汉译

▶ 对话 1   会展准备

制药厂的销售经理布莱克女士（B）准备在一个小型展览会上宣传她的产品。他正与辽通广告有限公司经理李先生（L）商谈此事。

B： 首先让我简要介绍一下我们公司的情况。我们是与加拿大合资经营的制药厂，是中国东北最大的制药厂之一。为了把我们公司的一种最新研制的药品推销到市场上去，我们考虑参加下个月在本市举行的一个小型展会，不知你们是否有兴趣助我们一臂之力。

L： 我们很乐意帮忙。能否先把您想要的东西告诉我，看看我们能在哪些方面帮上你们。

B： 首先，我们想要你们帮助我们做一些写有宣传标语的气球，给我们提供工作人员，等等。

L： 没有问题。我们有这类装备，我们还有礼仪小姐负责接待礼仪活动和一些讲解人员负责讲解和宣传贵方产品。

B： 很好，为了能让人们更好地了解我们的展示，我准备了一些明确易懂的中英文说明书。我们想请你们把它设计得更加生动和引人注目。

L： 小事一桩，这是我们的工作。我们肯定能做好。我们建议你在地方报纸上刊登广告，并张贴海报，向公众广泛告知展销会事宜。

B： 好建议。另外，我们想从本地各大医院聘请一些知名医生帮助我们进行义诊和咨询活动。你能否列一下可能受邀的医生的名单？

L： 这个主意不错，我会考虑联系他们的。

▶ 对话 2   在中国陶艺展上

展厅里，一位中国陶瓷制造商（C）正在和一位美国人（A）交谈。

A： 你们制作的陶瓷作品真美！

C： 我跟我父亲学习陶艺。然后，我又在学校攻读陶瓷工程学。

A： 看来你的心血没有白费。

C： 没错，我现在拥有 50 名员工。我希望能成为中国最大的陶瓷出口商。

A： 嗯，我们国内对陶瓷的需求量愈来愈大。

C： 是的，我们大部分产品销往美国。

A: 贵国陶瓷业的发展确实不同凡响。你们延续了古老的传统，同时又与现代科技一同进步。

C: 是的，我们在这方面的研究已经有了不错的成果。也很感激贵国技术人员的协助。

A: 给我介绍一下你们的设计吧。

C: 您觉得这个如何？

A: 很美。

C: 这是个 8 尺高的装饰花瓶。完全手工制造，而且镶嵌部分设计采用蚀镂法刻入。制造过程耗时 45 天，零售价为 3 000 美元。

A: 这样的成品确实值得这番功夫。这个式样呢？

C: 这个花瓶还在试验阶段。

A: 为什么？

C: 这个式样的制造成本相当高，而且因为体积小，顾客看到这样高的价钱就裹足不前。我们想如果售价降低，将能卖出更多。

A: 嗯，你可不能在质量上动手脚。美国顾客就是看上了中国陶瓷的高质量。

C: 正因为如此，降低价格的同时不能以牺牲质量为代价。

A: 嗯，谢谢你为我展示这些美丽的陶艺品。你们的设计和产品质量让我印象深刻。

▶ 对话 3　在前往电子产品展览会的路上

林小姐（L）正在机场候机大厅等候去芝加哥的飞机，这时她看到她旁边的一位男士（B）正在看一本电子产品杂志，于是她走上前去开始和他交谈。

L: 打扰了，我看到你看电子产品的杂志。你知不知道，明天在芝加哥有一个很大的电子产品展销会。

B: 当然知道啊！我就是为了这个才去芝加哥的。我叫巴尼·米勒，你呢？

L: 小林，中国五弗斯公司业务代表。你是不是很想参加这个展销会？

B: 嗯，我 3 个多月前就等着要来看了，此次将有 40 多个国家的厂商来参展。

L: 是呀，我真想瞧瞧明年将要上市的新产品。

B: 我倒比较想知道在电子工业中有什么新发现。

L: 是吗？可不可以告诉我，你是从事哪一方面的业务呢？

B: 当然可以。我在洛杉矶一家公司的研发部门工作，我们公司专门制造打印机。

L: 贵公司如何称呼？我可能听说过。

B: 不会吧，我们只是一家小公司而已，叫"HALCYON"。

L: 嗯……，你们在去年纽约的展销会上是不是推出一款小型，却属于高科技层次的打印机？

B: 对呀！那种型号成为我们去年最畅销的机种，只不过我们公司的名字却没人记得。

L: 我的任务之一就是找出最有潜力的产品及它们成功的原因，所以我可不是光记大公司的名字呢！

B: 我喜欢你这种态度。小林，到芝加哥后，咱们一块儿吃晚饭，再多谈一谈，你觉得怎么样？

▶ 对话 4 预订展位

瑞秋（R）到展中心来预订展位，会展中心服务人员菲利普（P）接待了她。

R: 早上好，先生！我来为我们公司预订一个展位，这是我的名片。请问还剩下多少展位？

P: 我还有几个人流量大的好地点。不过它们很快就会销售一空。*（展示会场平面图）* 这个角落的摊位怎样？它非常接近主要入口。

R: 我看一定很贵。我们只要靠近我们的主要竞争对手就好。他们的摊位设在哪里？

P: 有些还没有确认，不过他们大都在这个区域。

R: C322 摊位看起来是个很不错的点。

P: 这很接近洗手间。人流量很大，才 2 000 美元。

R: 那很贵啊！去年我们才付大约一半的价钱。

P: 不过，我们今年得给一个基本价，让大家日子好过些，而且我们预计参观人数会增加 15%。

R: 那么，这个方案中就不包括佣金和入场费提成了吧？

P: 没错。而且我们也加快行销计划的进度。你注意到《泰晤士报》上的广告了吗？

R: 是的，我的确看到了。那么，信用卡刷卡机和联网呢？

P: 和去年一样，需要额外加收 50 美元。

R: 好吧，那我们就订 C322 摊位。

Extended Reading

Strategic Trade-Fair Selection: SMES Must Choose Carefully

How do managers of SMEs decide which trade fairs to attend? What should they consider before allocating sizable investments in staff time and financial costs?

There are tricky questions, complicated by countless new exhibitions competing with each other throughout Asia and around the world.

For example, Beijing, Hong Kong, Singapore, Sydney and Bangkok all stage hotel-and-tourism events. Which should a small hotel group attend?

Huge wine shows take place in Hong Kong, Beijing, Tokyo and Singapore, not to mention significant producer shows in Australia which is best for a small distributor seeking new customers.

In 2000, 82,397 buyers (up 68% on 2000) and 3,061 exhibitors (up 50%) from the Chinese mainland attended trade fairs in Hong Kong. Mainland enterprises show a powerful preference for events in Hong Kong.

Despite huge advances allowing buyers to examine and source new products on the Internet, the amazing range and number of exhibitions keeps growing. Why?

Hong Kong Exporters' Association committee member Jeffery Lam says traders like doing business face-to-face. "Exhibitions are enjoyable and effective platforms for international buyers and sellers to make contract. They remain a superior medium because of the high concentration of a target audience. At a specialized fair, every single person walking the aisles is a potential customer," he says.

For three generations, Lam's family business, Forward Winsome Industries Ltd., has operated globally, making toys and gifts.

"There are so many trade-fair choices you simply cannot afford to attend them all. It is vital to pick the one with the right theme. The next most important consideration is traffic flow, without visitor traffic, there are no buyers," Lam says.

Paper communications president Leung Tin Fu stresses effectiveness. Anyone participating in a business exhibition is not merely going on a trip for a few days. "For good results, the process involves making long term plans," he says.

Paper communications participates in more than 10 exhibitions per year in Hong Kong, on the Chinese mainland and in Vietnam, Thailand, Malaysia and Indonesia.

"If you want to take products with you to an overseas exhibition, think about transportation and customs restrictions. Then plan the booth decoration and product presentation," Leung says.

"Most importantly, you must be sure the organizer is reliable and can attract quality supplies and visitors. Investigate this before making and advance payment."

Topic discussion:

1. Before attending the Exhibition, what factors should be taken into consideration?

2. What is the most decisive factor that you decide to attend an exhibition?

其他常用词汇和短语

adjustable standard　一种可以在其上随意安装展板的展架立杆

agent　*n.*　代理，代办处

air freight　空运货物

airway bill/air bill　（货物）空运单

aisle　*n.*　观众人行过道或通道

aisle signs　悬挂于展厅内用于标注过道名称或编号的过道标识

assembly　*v.*　展位搭建

attendance　*n.*　展览会人数

attendee　*n.*　展览会的参加者

attendee brochure　（发送给参观商或观众以吸引他们赴展览会参观的）参观商手册

back-wall booth　靠墙展位，边缘展位

bill of lading（B/L）　提单

blueprint　*n.*　展位设计施工图

bonded warehouse　保税仓库

bone yard　运输代理公司在展览现场所拥有或租用的用于存放展品空箱的仓库

booth area　摊位面积

booth number　摊位号

booth personnel　展台工作人员

booth sign　摊位楣板（用于标识参展商的名称、摊位号等）

booth size　展位尺寸

buying team　（公司）采购小组

carnet　*n.*　允许展品临时出口的海关批准文件

cartage　*n.*　货物运输费（或指展品从港口到展馆的短距离运输）

cash in advance（CIA）　预付

cash with order（CWO）　预订金

certificate of inspection　发运前对易变质物品等货物进行全面检查并证明其完好无损的证明文件

certificate of insurance　保险凭证

certificate of origin　原产地证明

consignee　*n.*　（展品）收货人

consumer show　面向公众开放的展览会，公共展

convention　*n.*　大型会议、展览或者两者兼而有之

corner booth　位于两个或两个以上人行通道交汇处的展位

customs　*n.*　海关

declared value　申报价格

dismantle　*v.*　撤展

display case　展示柜

display rules and regulations　展览会规则

dock　*n.*　码头

dock receipt　码头收货单据

double-decker　*n.*　双层展位（摊位）

double-faced panel　双面展板

drawback　*n.*　退税

drayage　*n.*　货运（专指把展品从码头运到展馆摊位及在展览会结束后把储存的空箱运到展台，并把回运展品再运到码头的运输业务）

drayage contractor　货运服务商

drayage form　货运申请表

duty　*n.*　关税

Unit

2

Inquiry, Offer and Counter-offer

询盘、报盘与还盘

Learning Resources

Warming-up

Usually, inquiry is an action undertaken by buyers to get the product information before purchasing. It is not only one of the most direct ways to acquire product details, but also a starting point of the formal contacts between buyers and sellers. When making an inquiry, besides the prices of goods, buyers may ask for more information, such as the specification, packing, delivery date and other forms. In an inquiry, buyers should clearly express what kind of information is needed and under what conditions the deal can be made, and it should be brief, specific, courteous and reasonable. In return, the answers to inquiries should be prompt, definite and helpful. Each inquiry is a sales opportunity, an opportunity to foster a potential long-term relationship.

In many types of business, it has always been the practice for the supplier to make an offer directly to his regular customers and to others who may be interested in his goods, without waiting for an inquiry. But when the supplier has received an inquiry from the buyers and decided to sell the goods, he should make an offer to him.

An offer is the expression of the wishes of sellers or buyers to sell or buy particular goods under stated terms (including quantity, price, time of shipment, terms of payment, etc.). Offers that can result in actual sales are vital for business transactions. According to their finality, offers used to be divided into two types: definite offer (or firm offer) and indefinite offer (non firm offer).

A counter-offer is an offer made by an offeree to an offeror, accepting some terms and changing other terms. It can be made verbally or in writing. In fact, a counter-offer is a partial rejection of the original offer. It is a new offer, at the same time, the original offer lapses. The buyer may not agree on the price, or packing, or shipment put before him by the seller of offeror, and state his own terms instead. Such alterations indicate that business has to be negotiated on the renewed basis. The original offeror or the seller now becomes the offeree and he has a right to accept or refuse. In making a counter-offer, one should express regret at inability to accept, explain reasons for non-acceptance and suggest that there may be other opportunities to do business together in future.

Dialogues

Dialogue 1 **Making an Inquiry about Computers**

At Vancouver summer show, the Canadian businessman Felix Smith (S) makes an inquiry about medium-sized computers made in China. Miss Han Fangfang (H) receives him.

H: Hello, do you want to take a look at our display?

S: I just went around. I'm interested in your computers. Do you have any literature that I can take with me?

H: Yes, here you are. And here is a series of catalogues of our latest models.

S: Umm, our company is interested in the medium-sized computers. Here is our purchase list.

H: I think all the models in Catalogue B, that's the green page catalogue, will meet your requirements in the purchase list.

S: Could you give us some idea about your prices?

H: Here is our price list for the medium-sized computers. The quotations are all FOB prices in US dollars. I'm sure you'll find our prices are most favorable.

S: I must tell you that your price is not favorable, a bit higher than some of the quotations I have received somewhere.

H: Yes, only a little bit higher. But everybody in the computer trade knows that our machines are of top quality.

S: They are, but we simply cannot order them at this price.

H: How many do you want to order?

S: 80 sets.

H: If you buy one hundred sets, we would reduce our price by 5 percent, to the level lower than any other sources. How about that?

S: OK. Let's make it a deal.

Dialogue 2 **Making an Offer about Toys and Dolls**

An American company wants to import some toys and dolls from China. Mr. Baker (B), the representative of the American side, was sent to Shanghai to hold a business talk. Miss. Li (L)

from Shanghai Toys Import and Export Corporation makes an offer.

L: Look, all these articles are our best selling lines.

B: Oh, how marvelous! Please give me two samples each of the toy car and the doll. What prices do you quote for these two items?

L: They are all on the catalogues. Here's the price list. You will see all the prices are very competitive.

B: Do you quote CIF or FOB?

L: All prices are FOB with a commission of five percent for you.

B: But I'd rather have your lowest quotation CIF 5% San Francisco.

L: That can be done easily. We'll work out CIF price this evening and give it to you tomorrow morning. But could you give us a rough idea of the quantity you require?

B: I think it's better for you to quote your price first. The size of our order depends very much on your price.

L: All right. We'll see what we can do.

B: How long do you generally keep your orders open?

L: The prices on the catalogue are without engagement. In case of firm offers we usually keep our offers open for three days.

B: Could you make the offers firm for seven days? You see, I'll have to send a telegram to my customers and ask about their opinions.

L: We'll consider it when we come to the concrete business.

▶ Dialogue 3 Negotiating a Counter-offer

Mr. Green (G), an American businessman, came to Ms. Li's (L) office to negotiate the price of the ball-point pen. Ms. Li makes the counter-offer and Mr. Green thinks the price Ms. Li quoted is much higher than he expected.

G: Hello, Ms. Li! I'm anxious to know your counter-offer.

L: Well, Mr. Green, we've got it for you. Now, here it is. For "The Hero 310" ball-point pen, our counter-offer is as follows: US$6 dozen CIF New York.

G: My goodness! At that price we are not playing in the same ball park.

L: We are sincere. My counter-offer is in line with the international market.

G: We are also sincere about doing business with you, but the difference between your counter-offer and our price is too wide.

L: Business is rather slow nowadays. And the competition for the market is rather keen. For instance, South Korea has just joined in, and the offer they make is much lower than the one you have quoted.

G: But our product has so far enjoyed better quality than others. Considering the quality, I should say the price we offered is reasonable.

L: No doubt your product is of high quality, but your price still shouldn't be so high. To be frank, there is too much water in your price.

G: What are you talking about? I don't understand you.

L: I mean you didn't quote us a firm offer. We have to squeeze the water out of your price so as to get to the rock-bottom price.

G: I definitely don't agree with you. As you know, the price for raw materials has gone up in recent years, so if we accept your counter-offer, we will lose money. Anyhow, we can't reduce the price to the level you want.

L: Now how much can you bring down the price?

G: In order to conclude business, we can give you a special discount of 3%. That's really the best we can do.

L: Good! That's the first step. Now, could you give us 1% more discount if our order is substantial?

G: But what's your idea of a substantial order?

L: Well, supposing our order is 10,000 dozen.

G: Though your order can hardly be called substantial, for a good start to our business relationship, we will agree to reduce altogether 4% of the price we quoted, that is US$5.76 CIF New York.

L: Done. I'm very glad we have finally brought the transaction to a successful conclusion.

G: Me too.

▶ **Dialogue 4** **A Discussion on the Price after the Counter-offer**

After receiving an offer from Mr. Zhang (Z), sales representative of a Chinese company, the Canadian dealer, Mr. Hawk (H), makes a counter-offer. Then the two parties hold further discussions on the price issue.

H: Frankly speaking, I think the price is working against us.

Z: What leads you to think so? Tell me candidly, Mr. Hawk.

H: I look at it this way. Supplies should be able to reduce their CIF price, even lower than their home price.

Z: We offer you on the same basis as we quote in the domestic market.

H: That's the point. Your overhead is in your domestic price, but it can not be carried in the CIF price.

Z: But even with the overhead out, the export overhead must be put in. Finally, it comes to the same thing.

H: But we still think the price is too high for us to accept. To conclude the business, I'm afraid you have to reduce your price by about eight percent.

Z: Eight percent? That is impossible. How can you expect us to reduce our price to such an extent?

H: Then how about six percent? This is the highest we can accept. If anything higher than this, we will give up the deal.

Z: Well, allow me to study it for a couple of days.

Words and Expressions

inquiry *n.* 询盘，询价	meet one's requirement 满足要求
offer *n. & v.* 报盘	quotation *n.* 报价
counter-offer *n.* 还盘	favorable *a.* 优惠的
display *n.* 展示，展览，陈列	make it a deal 成交
literature *n.* [总称]（商品说明	concrete *a.* 具体的，有形的
书之类的）印刷品	candidly *ad.* 坦诚地，率直地，直率而
medium-sized computer 中型计算机	诚恳地
purchase list 采购单	overhead *n.* 经常费用，开销
a series of 一系列	

Notes

1. 询盘

询盘（inquiry）是一件技巧性的商务工作。询盘既要发给多个供货商，但又不可以滥发。多方询盘可获得多方的信息，可有所比较，选择有利者。滥发容易引起供货商哄抬物价。因此，询盘时既要充分考虑供货商及其地区的情况，又要对其产生诱惑，使其感受商机。要想达到有效的询盘，很多公司采用寄发印制好的询盘表，这种形式简单明了，直奔主题。作为一个未来的购买者，询盘人应该简单明了地说明其兴趣所在。作为一个初始询盘人，他应该获得对方的充分了解；作为一个具体的询盘人，他应该对想要的商品进行详细说明，以使供货商采取具体的行动。

2. 报盘

报盘（offer），也叫报价，是卖方主动向买方提供商品信息，或者是对询盘的答复，是卖方根据买方的来信，向买方报盘，其内容可包括商品名称、规格、数量、包装条件、价格、付款方式和交货期限等。报盘有以下两种。

（1）虚盘（non-firm offers），即无约束力的报盘。一般情况下，多数报盘均为虚盘，虚盘不规定报盘的有效日期，并且附有保留条件，如："The offer is subject to our final confirmation/prior sale."（该报盘以我方最后确认/事先售出为准。）。

（2）实盘（firm offers），即规定有效日期的报盘，而且实盘一旦被接受，报盘人就不能撤回。

3. 还盘

还盘（counter offer）是交易方式之一，即接盘人对所接发盘表示接受，但对其内容提出更改的行为。还盘实质上构成对原发盘的某种程度的拒绝，也是接盘人以发盘人的名义所提出的新发盘。因此，一经还盘，原发盘即失效，新发盘取代它成为交易谈判的基础。如果另一方对还盘内容不同意，还可以进行反还盘（或称再还盘）。还盘可以在双方之间反复进行，还盘的内容通常仅陈述需变更或增添的条件，对双方同意的交易条件则无须重复。在国际贸易中，往往经过多次的还盘、反还盘，才最终达成协议。

受盘人在接到发盘后，不能完全同意发盘的内容，为了进一步磋商交易，对发盘提出修改意见，用口头或书面形式表示出来，就构成还盘。

4. FOB

FOB（free on board）也称"离岸价"。按 FOB 术语成交，由买方负责派船接运货物，卖方应在合同规定的装运港和规定的期限内，将货物装上买方指定的船只，并及时通知买方。货物在装船时越过船舷，风险即由卖方转移至买方。

在 FOB 条件下，卖方要负担风险和费用，领取出口许可证或其他官方证件，并负责办理出口手续。采用 FOB 术语成交时，卖方还要自费提供证明其已按规定完成交货义务的证件。如果该证件并非运输单据，在买方要求并由买方承担风险和费用的情况下，卖方可以给予协助以取得提单或其他运输单据。

一些国家鼓励出口使用 CIF 术语，进口使用 FOB 术语，由本国保险公司和承运人保险或承运。

5. CIF

CIF（cost, insurance and freight）的中译名为"成本加保险费加运费"。按此术

语成交，货价的构成因素中包括从装运港至约定目的港的通常运费和约定的保险费，故卖方除具有与 CFR 术语相同的义务外，还要为买方办理货运保险，交付保险费。按一般国际贸易惯例，卖方投保的保险金额应按 CIF 价加成 10%。如买卖双方未约定具体险别，则卖方只需取得最低限度的保险险别，如买方要求加保战争险，在保险费由买方负担的前提下，卖方应予加保。卖方投保时，如能办到，应以合同货币投保。

需要强调的是，按 CIF 术语成交，虽然由卖方安排货物运输和办理货运保险，但卖方并不承担保证把货送到约定目的港的义务，因为 CIF 是属于装运交货的术语，而不是目的港交货的术语。

按照规定，CIF 术语只能适用于海运和内河航运，如要求卖方先将货物交到港口货站，以及使用滚装/滚卸或集装箱运输时，则使用 CIP 术语更为适宜。

在我国出口贸易中，按 CIF 条件成交的较为普遍。为了正确运用 CIF 术语，应特别注意下列事项。

（1）必须认真核算运费。

按 CIF 条件成交时，由于货价构成因素中包括运费，故卖方对外报价时，应认真核算运费，把运费因素考虑到货价中去。那种不分销售地区，不分距离远近，都按同一价格出售的做法，显然是不合适的。

卖方核算运费时，主要应考虑下列因素。

① 运输距离的远近。同一种货物，如运输距离不同，其运输费用的多少也必然有别，所以在按 CIF 条件成交时，应当核算运输成本，以体现地区差价。

② 是否需要转船。一般来说，直达运输比中转运输的费用低，所以按 CIF 条件成交时，应考虑是否需要转船。在成交量少而又无直达班轮运输的情况下，货物必须中途转船运输，这势必增加一笔转船的费用，此项费用也应计入运输成本并考虑到货价中去。在 CIF 条件下，不考虑转船与否，都按同一价格出售的不计成本的做法，也是不合理的。

③ 运价变动的趋势。买卖双方按 CIF 条件成交时，在确定货价的同时，应考虑市场运价变动趋势及各种附加费，把运价变动的风险计算到货价中去，以避免出现只顾成交、不顾运输和只管货价、不管运价的偏向。

（2）必须正确理解和处理风险与保险的关系。

风险和保险是既有联系又有区别的两个不同的概念。在 CIF 条件下，买方应承担货物在运输途中的风险，买方为了转嫁风险，应向保险公司办理保险。但买方为了省事，在洽商交易时，要求卖方代办保险，并商定保险费计入货价中。由于 CIF 货价中包括保险费，故卖方必须约定条件自费办理保险，卖方为买方利益所进行的这种保险，纯属代办性质，如果事后发生承保损失，由买方凭卖方提交的保险单直接向保险公司索赔，能否索赔到手，卖方概不负责。

（3）必须明确大宗商品交易下的卸货费由何方负担。

在国际贸易中，大宗商品通常洽租不定期船运输。大多数情况下，船舶公司承运大宗货物，一般是不负担装卸费的。因此，在 CIF 条件下，买卖双方容易在卸货费由何方负责的问题上引起争议。为了明确责任，买卖双方应在合同中就卸货费由谁负担的问题做出明确具体的规定。

当买方不愿负担卸货费时，在商订合同时，可要求在 CIF 后加列"liner terms"（班轮条件）、"landed"（卸到岸上）或"under ship's tackle"（船舶吊钩下交货）字样。

当卖方不愿负担卸货时，在商订合同时，可要求在 CIF 后加列"ex ship's hold"（舱底交货）字样。

上述 CIF 后加列的各种附加条件，如同 CFR 后加列各种条件一样，只是为了明确卸货费由谁负担，它并不影响交货地点和风险转移的界线。

（4）必须搞好单证工作。

按照对 CIF 术语的传统解释，CIF 属象征性交货，卖方负有向买主提交约定的装运单据的义务，买方则负有凭装运单据付款的义务。也就是说，在 CIF 条件下，买方是凭单据和付款对流的原则，因此，即使在卖方装船以后至交单这段时间内，货物发生灭失或损坏，只要卖方提交的单据符合要求，买方就不得拒收单据和拒付货款，而只能先付未赎单，然后凭所取得的有关单据向船方或保险公司提出索赔，追回损失。因此，CIF 交易实际上是一种单据买卖。

由此可见，装运单据在 CIF 交易中具有特别重要的意义，所以在实际工作中应重视和搞好单证工作。当然，CIF 是单据买卖的说法，并不意味着可以因此而减轻卖方交货方面的责任。CIF 的卖方，除应提交约定的装运单据外，还应保证交运约定的货物。

6. How long do you generally keep your orders open?

   一般你们的报盘有效期是多久？

7. My counter-offer is in line with the international market.

   我方的还价和目前国际市场水平是一致的。

8. …we are not playing in the same ball park.

   ……咱俩可谈不到一块儿。

9. Business is rather slow nowadays. And the competition for the market is rather keen.

   近来市场冷淡，而竞争异常激烈。

10. To be frank, there is too much water in your price.

    坦诚地说，你方报价水分不少。

11. We have to squeeze the water out of your price so as to get to the rock-bottom price.

    我方必须将你方价格中的水分挤去，以便见到实价。

Useful Sentences

● **Sentences for making an inquiry**

1. Heavy enquiries witness the quality of our products.
   大量询盘证明我们产品质量过硬。

2. As soon as the price picks up, enquiries will revive.
   一旦价格回升，询盘将恢复活跃。

3. Enquiries for carpets are getting more numerous.
   对地毯的询盘日益增加。

4. Enquiries are so large that we can only allot you 200 cases.
   询盘如此之多，我们只能分给你们 200 箱货。

5. Enquiries are dwindling.
   询盘正在减少。

6. Enquiries are dried up.
   询盘正在绝迹。

7. They promised to transfer their future enquiries to Chinese corporations.
   他们答应将以后的询盘转给中国公司。

8. Generally speaking, inquiries are made by the buyers.
   询盘一般由买方发出。

9. Mr. Baker is sent to Beijing to make an inquiry at China National Textiles Corporation.
   贝克先生来北京向中国纺织公司进行询价。

10. We regret that the goods you inquire about are not available.
    很遗憾，你们所询的货物现在无货。

11. In the import and export business, we often make inquiries at foreign suppliers.
    在进出口交易中，我们常向外商询价。

12. To make an inquiry about our oranges, a representative of the Japanese company paid us a visit.
    为了对我们的橙子询价，那家日本公司的一名代表访问了我们。

13. We cannot take care of your enquiry at present.
    我们现在无力顾及你方的询盘。

14. Your enquiry is too vague to enable us to reply you.
    你们的询盘不明确，我们无法答复。

15. Now that we've already made an inquiry about your articles, will you please reply as soon as possible?

既然我们已经对你们的产品进行询价，可否尽快给予答复？

16. China National Silk Corporation received the inquiry sheet sent by a British company.

中国丝绸公司收到了英国一家公司的询价单。

17. Thank you for your inquiry.

谢谢你们的询价。

18. May I have an idea of your prices?

可以了解一下你们的价格吗？

19. Can you give me an indication of price?

你能给我一个估价吗？

20. Please let us know your lowest possible prices for the relevant goods.

请告知你们有关商品的最低价。

21. If your prices are favorable, I can place the order right away.

如果你们的价格优惠，我们可以马上订货。

22. When can I have your firm CIF prices, Mr. Li?

李先生，什么时候能得到你们到岸价的实盘？

23. We'd rather have you quote us FOB price.

我们希望你们报离岸价格。

24. Would you tell us your best prices CIF Hamburg for the chairs.

请告知你方椅子至汉堡到岸价的最低价格。

25. Will you please tell the quantity you require so as to enable us to sort out the offers?

为了便于我方报价，可以告诉我们你们所要的数量吗？

26. We'd like to know what you can offer as well as your sales conditions.

我们想了解你们能供应什么，以及你们的销售条件。

27. How long does it usually take you to make delivery?

你们通常要多久才能交货？

28. Could you make prompt delivery?

可以即期交货吗？

29. Would you accept delivery spread over a period of time?

不知你们能否接受在一段时间里分批交货？

30. Could you tell me which kind of payment terms you'll choose?

能否告知你们将采用哪种付款方式？

31. Will you please tell us the earliest possible date you can make shipment?

你能否告知我们最早的船期？

32. Do you take special orders?
   你们接受特殊订货吗？

33. Could you please send us a catalog of your rubber boots together with terms of payment?
   你能给我们寄来一份胶靴的目录，连同告诉我们付款方式吗？

34. He inquired about the varieties, specifications and price, and so on and so forth.
   他询问了品种、规格和价格等情况。

35. We have inquired of Manager Zhang about the varieties, quality and price of tea.
   我们向张经理询问了茶叶的品种、质量和价格等问题。

36. We have the offer ready for you.
   我们已经为你准备好报盘了。

37. I come to hear about your offer for fertilizers.
   我来听听你们有关化肥的报盘。

38. Please make us a cable offer.
   请来电报报盘。

39. Please make an offer for the bamboo shoots of the quality as that in the last contract.
   请把上次合同中订的那种质量的竹笋向我们报个价。

40. We are in a position to offer tea from stock.
   我们现在可以报库存现有茶叶的价格。

41. We'll try our best to get a bid from the buyers.
   我们一定尽力获得买主的递价。

42. We'll let you have the official offer next Monday.
   下星期就给您正式报盘。

43. I'm waiting for your offer.
   我正等您的报价呢。

44. We can offer you a quotation based upon the international market.
   我们可以按国际市场价格给您报价。

45. We have accepted your firm offer.
   我们已收到了你们报的实盘。

46. We offer firm for reply 11 a.m. tomorrow.
   我们报实盘，以明天上午 11 点答复为有效。

47. We'll let you have our firm offer next Sunday.
   下星期日我们就向你们发实盘。

48. We're willing to make you a firm offer at this price.
   我们愿意以此价格为你们报实盘。

● **Sentences for making an offer**

1. Our offer is RMB300 per set of tape-recorder, FOB Tianjin.
   我们的报价是每台录音机 300 元人民币，天津离岸价。

2. We quote this article at $250 per M/T C&F.
   我们报成本加运费价每吨 250 美元。

3. My offer was based on reasonable profit, not on wild speculations.
   我的报价以合理利润为依据，不是漫天要价。

4. We have received offers recently, most of which are below $100.
   我们最近的报价大多数都在 100 美元以下。

5. Moreover, we've kept the price close to the cost of production.
   再说，我们的价格已经很接近生产成本了。

6. I think the price we offered you last week is the best one.
   相信我上周的报价是最好的。

7. No other buyers have bid higher than this price.
   没有别的买主的出价高于此价。

8. The price you offered is above previous prices.
   你方的报价高于上次。

9. It was a higher price than we offered to other suppliers.
   此价格比我们给其他供货人的出价要高。

10. We can't accept your offer unless the price is reduced by 5%.
    除非你们减价 5%，否则我们无法接受报盘。

11. I'm afraid I don't find your price competitive at all.
    我看你们的价格毫无任何竞争力。

12. Let me make you a special offer.
    我给你一个特别优惠价。

13. We'll give you the preference of our offer.
    我们将优先向你们报盘。

14. I should have thought my offer was reasonable.
    我本以为我的报价是合理的。

15. You'll see that our offer compares favorably with the quotations you can get elsewhere.
    你会发现我们的报价比别处要便宜。

16. This offer is based on an expanding market and is competitive.
    此报盘着眼于扩大销路而且很有竞争力。

17. Our offers are for 3 days.

我们的报盘三天有效。

18. We have extended the offer as per your request.
    我们已按你方要求将报盘延期。

19. The offer holds good until 5 o'clock p.m. June 22, 2015, Beijing time.
    报价有效期到北京时间 2015 年 6 月 22 日下午 5 点。

20. All prices in the price lists are subject to our confirmation.
    报价单中所有价格以我方确认为准。

21. This offer is subject to your reply reaching here before the end of this month.
    该报盘以你方回复本月底前到达我地为有效。

22. This offer is subject to the goods being unsold.
    该报盘以商品未售出为准。

23. I'm afraid the offer is unacceptable.
    恐怕你方的报价不能接受。

24. The offer is not workable.
    报盘不可行。

25. The offer is given without engagement.
    报盘没有约束力。

26. It is difficult to quote without full details.
    未说明详尽细节难以报价。

27. Buyers do not welcome offers made at wide intervals.
    买主不喜欢报盘间隔太久。

28. We cannot make any headway with your offer.
    以你们的报盘，恐怕我们（之间的贸易）无法取得进展。

29. Please renew your offer for two days further.
    请将报盘延期两天。

30. Please renew your offer on the same terms and conditions.
    请按同样的条件恢复报盘。

31. We regret we have to decline your offer.
    很抱歉，我们不得不拒绝你方报盘。

32. The offer is withdrawn.
    该报盘已经撤回。

33. We prefer to withhold offers for a time.
    我们宁愿暂停报盘。

34. Buyers are worried at the lack of offer.
    买主因无报盘而苦恼。

● **Sentences for making a counter-offer**

1. Let's have you counter-offer.
   请还个价。

2. Do you want to make a counter-offer?
   您是否还个价？

3. I appreciate your counter-offer but find it too low.
   谢谢您的还价，可我觉得太低了。

4. Now we look forward to replying to our offer in the form of counter-offer.
   现在我们希望你们能以还盘的形式对我方的报盘予以答复。

5. Your price is too high to interest buyers in counter-offer.
   你的价格太高，买方没有兴趣还盘。

6. Your counter-offer is much more modest than mine.
   你们的还盘比我的要保守得多。

7. We make a counter-offer to you of $150 per metric ton FOB London.
   我们还价为每公吨伦敦离岸价 150 美元。

8. I'll respond to your counter-offer by reducing our price by three dollars.
   我同意你们的还价，减价 3 美元。

9. Business is closed at this price.
   交易就按此价敲定。

10. Your price is acceptable (unacceptable).
    你方的价格可以（不可以）接受。

11. Your price is feasible (infeasible).
    你方的价格是可行（不可行）的。

12. Your price is workable.
    你方的出价可行。

13. Your price is realistic (unrealistic).
    你方的价格合乎实际（不现实）。

14. Your price is reasonable (unreasonable).
    你方的价格合理（不合理）。

15. Your price is practicable (impracticable).
    你方的价格是行得通（行不通）的。

16. Your price is attractive (not attractive).
    你方的价格有吸引力（无吸引力）。

17. Your price is inducing (not inducing).

你方的价格有吸引力（无吸引力）。

18. Your price is convincing (not convincing).
    你方的价格有说服力（无说服力）。

19. Your price is competitive (not competitive).
    你方的价格有竞争力（无竞争力）。

20. The goods are (not) competitively priced.
    此货物的定价有（无）竞争力。

21. Price is turning high (low).
    价格上涨（下跌）。

22. Price is high (low).
    价格高（低）。

23. Price is rising (falling).
    价格上升（下降）。

24. Price is up (down).
    价格上涨（下跌）。

25. Price is looking up.
    价格看涨。

26. Price has skyrocketed.
    价格猛涨。

27. Price has shot up.
    价格飞涨。

28. Price has risen perpendicularly.
    价格直线上升。

29. Price has risen in a spiral.
    价格螺旋上升。

30. Price has hiked.
    价格急剧抬高。

31. Your price is on the high side.
    你方的价格偏高。

32. Price has advanced.
    价格已上涨。

33. The goods are priced too high.
    货物定价太高。

34. Your price is rather stiff.
    你方的价格相当高。

35. Price is leveling off.

价格趋平。

36. Your price is prohibitive.

你方的价格高得令人望而却步。

37. The Japanese yen is strengthening.

日元坚挺。

38. The US dollar is weakening.

美元疲软。

39. Your price is much higher than the price from UK, France and Germany.

你方的价格比英、法、德的都高。

40. Since the prices of the raw materials have been raised, I'm afraid that we have to adjust the prices of our products accordingly.

由于原材料价格上涨，我们不得不对产品的价格做相应的调整。

41. Your price is $500 per MT, twice that of the other countries.

你们每公吨 500 美元的价格是其他国家的两倍。

42. Is it possible for you to raise (lift) the price by 5%?

你们能否把价格提高 5%？

43. Price is hovering between $5 and $8.

价格徘徊于 5 至 8 美元之间。

44. We regret we have to maintain our original price.

很遗憾我们不得不保持原价。

45. Price is easy.

价格疲软。

46. Price is easy off.

价格趋于疲软。

47. Price has declined.

价格已跌落。

48. Price has dipped (sagged).

价格已下降。

49. It simply can't stand such a big cut.

再也经不住大幅度削价了。

50. Price has tobogganed.

价格急剧下降。

51. Price has plummeted.

价格暴跌。

52. Price has downslided.
    价格剧降。

53. This new product is moderately priced.
    新产品的定价适度。

54. Articles for everyday use are economically priced.
    日用品价格低廉。

55. Everyone knows, the price of crude oil has greatly decreased.
    人人皆知，目前原油价格大幅度下跌。

56. We've already cut the price to the minimum.
    我们已将价格减至最低限度了。

57. The French price of stainless steel plates is about $1,200 per MT, while the German price is still lower.
    法国的不锈钢板价格为每公吨 1 200 美元，德国的还要低。

58. We're ready to reduce the price by 5%.
    我们准备减价百分之五。

59. To have this business concluded, you need to lower your price at least by 3%.
    为达成这笔交易，你方应至少减价 3%。

60. Business is possible if you can lower the price to HK$2,150.
    你方若能减价到 2 150 港元，可能成交。

61. The utmost (best) we can do is to reduce the price by 2%.
    我们最多能减价百分之二。

62. We cannot take anything off the price.
    我们不能再降价了。

63. We've already cut down our prices to cost level.
    我们已经将价格降到成本费用的水平了。

64. There is no room for any reduction in price.
    价格上毫无再减的余地了。

65. Our rock-bottom price is $500 per MT, and cannot be further lowered.
    我们的最低价是每公吨 500 美元，不能再低了。

66. DM210 is equivalent to RMB 400.
    210 德国马克折合人民币 400 元。

67. Don't you wish to employ RMB of ours? US dollars might be adopted.
    如果你们不同意用我们的人民币结算，美元也可以。

68. Are you afraid of losing money due to exchange rate fluctuations?
    您是不是怕由于汇率浮动而吃亏？

69. I can give you a definite answer on the price terms.
我可以就价格条件明确答复你方。

70. You wish to have a discussion about the price terms of washers.
您是想谈谈洗衣机的价格条件吧。

71. Yes, all of the price terms are acceptable.
是的，所有的价格条件都是可以接受的。

72. CIF is the price term normally adopted by you, right?
CIF 是你们经常采用的价格条件，是吗？

73. Sometimes FOB and C&F are also employed.
我们有时也用离岸价或成本加运费价。

74. You said yesterday that the price was $60 per MT, CIF Brussels.
您昨天说价格定为每公吨 60 英镑 CIF 布鲁塞尔。

75. In case FOB is used, risks and charges are to be passed over to the buyers once the cargo is put on board the ship.
如果采用离岸价，货物一越过船舷，货物的风险和费用就都转给买方了。

76. Your price is quoted C&F Xingang at DM200 per washer, right?
你方的报价是每台洗衣机 200 德国马克，C&F 新港价，对吗？

Exercises

I **Complete the following dialogues.**

1. **A:** Just one glance tells me that your price has been soaring! It's almost 20% higher than that of last year. _____.
   （按这种价格买进，我方实在难以推销。）

   B: I'm a little surprised to hear you say that. You know very well that the market has gone up a great deal recently. _____.
   （我们认为我方的报价已经是最低的了。）

2. **A:** _____.
   （我们将考虑你的建议，内部讨论一下。）

   B: Please do. _____.
   （希望给我方报优惠价。）

3. **A:** We are interested in your products. What about the supply position?
   B: _____.

（目录中大部分的货源都很充足。）

4. **A:** Is your offer a firm one or subject to your confirmation?

   B: _____.

   （实盘，有效期 3 天。）

5. **A:** What about the commission? From European suppliers I usually get a 3 to 5 percent commission for my imports. It's the general practice.

   B: As a rule we do not allow any commission. _____
   _____. （但是如果订货数量大，我们可以考虑。）

II Situational practice.

Make dialogues according to the following situations.

1. You represent a cosmetics company, and you are selling fat-reducing soap that is very popular in China. A businessman from the United States heard about your soap and wants to place a trial order. The discussion starts with an inquiry and proceeds to an offer. Your offer is $15 per dozen.

2. At a fair, you are selling green tea, which enjoys a great popularity. A businesswoman from Japan is very keen on it. Your offer is $25 per kilogram. The discussion starts with an inquiry and proceeds to an offer, and finally you decide on a price and date of delivery.

3. You are going to import a quantity of chemical fertilizers for your end-users. But you find the price quoted by Mr. Smith of a Canadian firm on the high side compared with the ruling prices on the world market. Taking advantage of a weak market that is unfavorable to sellers, you try your best to persuade Mr. Smith to reduce his price.

对话汉译

对话 1 对计算机的询盘

在温哥华夏展上，加拿大客商菲利克斯·史密斯（S）对中国制造的中型计算机进行询盘。韩芳芳小姐（H）接待了他。

H: 您好，要看看我们的展示吗？

S: 看过了，我对你们的计算机很感兴趣，你们有可以带走的资料吗？

H: 有的，给您。这是我们最新机型的产品目录。

S: 呃，我们公司对中型机感兴趣。这是我们的采购单。

H: 我认为产品目录 B，就是那本绿色产品目录上的机型，能满足采购单上的要求。

S: 能报一下价吗？

H: 这是中型机的价格单，所有的报价都是美元离岸价，我肯定您会发现我们的价格是最优惠的。

S: 我必须告诉您，你们的价格并不优惠，比我们从别处得到的报价要高一些。

H: 只是稍高一点，但计算机行业中的人们都知道我们的机器质量过硬。

S: 质量是好，但我们不能按这个价格订货。

H: 您打算订购多少？

S: 80 台。

H: 如果你方买 100 台，我们就给你们 5% 的优惠，低于其他厂家的价格。怎么样？

S: 好吧，成交！

▶ 对话 **2**　就玩具和洋娃娃报价

一家美国公司想从中国进口一些玩具和洋娃娃。美方代表贝克先生（B）被派到上海洽谈业务。上海玩具进出口公司的李小姐（L）向他报了价。

L: 瞧，这些商品都是我们的畅销货。

B: 啊，太棒了！请给我玩具汽车和洋娃娃各两件样品。对这些商品，你们报什么价？

L: 这都在我们的目录册上。这是价目表。你看，所有的价格都很优惠。

B: 你们的报价是到岸价还是离岸价？

L: 所有报价都是离岸价含你方佣金 5%。

B: 但我想要你们最低的旧金山到岸价，并含佣金 5%。

L: 这很好办。我们今天晚上定出到岸价来，明天上午给您。但您能否让我知道您大概要订的数量。

B: 我觉得最好还是你们先报价。我们订单的大小在很大程度上取决于你方的价格。

L: 那好吧。看我方能做些什么吧。

B: 一般你们的报盘有效期是多长？

L: 目录上的都是无约束价格。如果是实盘，我们通常保留有效期 3 天。

B: 你们能使报盘有效 7 天吗？你看，我必须得给我的客户们打电报询问一下他们的意见。

L: 谈到具体业务时我们会考虑的。

▶ 对话 **3**　就还盘展开商谈

美国商人格林先生（G）来到李女士（L）的办公室商谈圆珠笔的价格。李女士给格林先生做出了还盘，但是格林先生认为李女士的出价高出了他所期望的价格。

G: 你好，李女士！我很想知道你方的还盘情况。

L: 格林先生，我们已经为你方制定出了还盘，给你。英雄牌 310 圆珠笔的纽约到岸价是每打 6 美元。

G: 天啊！这样的价格，咱俩可谈不到一块儿。

L: 我方是认真的，我方的还价和目前国际市场水平是一致的。

G: 我们也是有诚意跟你们做成这笔生意的，但你方的还价与我方的价格相差太悬殊了。

L: 近来市场冷淡，况且竞争激烈。如你所知，韩国厂家最近也加入了竞争，他们提出的价格就比你方的价格低。

G: 迄今为止我方产品一直拥有比其他厂家的产品更好的质量，考虑到质量因素，我认为我方的价格是合理的。

L: 当然，你方产品的质量较高，但价格也不能因此就这样高啊！坦率地讲，你方报价水分不少。

G: 你说什么？我不明白你的意思。

L: 我的意思是说你方并未报给我方实盘，我方必须将你方价格中的水分挤掉，以便见到实价。

G: 我根本不同意你的这种说法。如你所知，近来原材料价格上涨得厉害，如果我们接受你方的还价，我们将亏损，我们无论如何不能把价格降低到你方还得那样低的水平上。

L: 那么，你方在价格上能降低多少呢？

G: 为了成交，我们可以给你方 3% 的特别折扣，我们确实只能到此为止了。

L: 很好，这是第一步。如果我方的订货数量相当大的话，你方能再给 1% 的折扣吗？

G: 那么你说的数量相当大是个什么概念呢？

L: 假如是 1 000 打呢？

G: 虽然这样的数量很难说得上相当大，但为了我们之间的业务关系有个良好的开端，我们同意对我方原始价格降低 4%，也就是说，纽约到岸价是 5.76 美元。

L: 成交。很高兴我们终于做成了这笔生意。

G: 我也一样。

▶ 对话 4　还盘后就价格问题进行磋商

收到中方公司销售代表张先生（Z）的发盘后，加拿大交易商霍克先生（H）做了还盘。然后，双方就价格问题进行了深入的磋商。

H: 说实在话，我认为这个价格对我们是行不通的。

Z: 是什么使您这样想呢？霍克先生，请您坦白地告诉我。

H: 我是这样认为的：供应商应该有能力降低他们的到岸价，甚至低于其国内价格。

Z: 我们的发盘与我们报给国内市场的是以同样的基准。

H: 问题就在这里。贵公司的经营费用包含在你们国内的价格里，但这项费用是不应该带入到岸价里的。

Z: 但即使排除经营费用，外销经营费用还是得加进去的，到最后其结果还是一样的。

H: 但我认为这么高的价格我们难以接受。为了达成交易，恐怕你们得降价 8%。

Z: 8%？这是不可能的！你们怎么可以要求我们把价格降到这个地步！

H: 那么，降低 6%怎么样？这是我们所能接受的最高价格了，高于这个价格，我们将放弃这笔交易。

Z: 哦，给我几天时间考虑一下。

Extended Reading

How to Inquire Effectively

Most letters of inquiry are short and simple, so much so that many firms have adopted the practice of sending printed inquiry forms, thereby eliminating the need for a letter. As a prospective buyer, the writer of an inquiry states briefly and clearly what he is interested in, and this is all the receiver of the letter needs to know. It is rather difficult when the object of your inquiry is to obtain a special price for regular orders, or selling rights in your area. In cases like these you are asking for concessions, and you have to "sell" your proposal to the supplier. This requires much more skill than the writing of a routine inquiry.

A first inquiry—a letter sent to a supplier with whom you have not previously done business should include the following information.

(1) A brief mention of how you obtained your potential supplier's name. Your source may be an embassy, consulate, or chamber of commerce; you may have seen the goods in question at an exhibition or trade fair; you may be writing as the result of a recommendation from a business associate, on the basis of an advertisement in the daily, weekly or trade press.

(2) Some indication of the demand in your area for the goods which the supplier deals with.

(3) Details of what you would like your prospective supplier to send you. Normally you will be interested in a catalogue, a price list, discounts, methods of payment, delivery times and samples.

How to Reply Inquiries Effectively

An inquiry received from abroad must be answered fully and promptly. If there is no stock available for the time being, you should acknowledge the inquiry at once, explaining the situation and assuring that you will revert to it once supply becomes available. If the inquiry is from an old customer, say how much you appreciate it. If it is from a new customer, say you are glad to receive it and express the hope of a lasting friendly business relationship so as to create good will and leave a good impression on the reader.

In a word, the reply to an inquiry should be prompt and courteous and cover all information asked for. It should be written in the following order.

(1) Thank the writer of the letter of inquiry.

(2) Supply all the information requested, and refer both to enclosures and to samples, catalogues and other items being sent by separate letters.

(3) Provide additional information, not specifically requested by the customer, so long as it is relevant.

(4) Conclude with one or two lines encouraging the customer to place orders and assuring them of good service.

Topic discussion:

1. What can make your inquiry more effective?
2. What can make your reply to inquiries more effective?

 其他常用词汇和短语

询盘：

an occasional inquiry　偶尔询盘

firm price　实价，实盘

inquire about　对……询价

inquirer　n.　询价者

inquiry sheet　询价单

keep inquiry in mind　记住询盘

make delivery　交货

make prompt delivery　即期交货

payment terms　付款方式，付款条件

sales conditions　销售条件

special orders　特殊订货

specific inquiry　具体询盘

报盘：

cable an offer/to telegraph an offer
　电报（进行）报价

competitive　a.　竞争的，有竞争
　性的

cost of production　生产费用

entertain an offer　考虑报盘

extend an offer　延长报盘

firm offer　实盘

forward an offer/to send an offer 寄送报盘

get an offer/to obtain an offer 获得……报盘

give an offer 给……报盘

make an offer for 对……报盘

non-firm offer 虚盘

offer and acceptance by post 通过邮政报价及接受

offer for 对……报盘（报价）

offer subject to export/import license 以获得出口（进口）许可证为准的报盘

offer subject to first available steamer 以装第一艘轮船为准的报盘

offer subject to goods being unsold 以商品未售出为准的报盘

offer subject to our final confirmation 以我方最后确认为准的报盘

offer subject to our written acceptance 以我方书面接受为准的报盘

offer subject to prior sale 以提前售出为准的报盘

offer subject to sample approval 以样品确定后生效为准的报盘

offer subject to your reply reaching here 以你方答复到达我地为准的报盘

official offer 正式报价（报盘）

preferential offer 优先报盘

reasonable a. 合理的

renew an offer/reinstate an offer 恢复报盘

subject to 以……为条件，以……为准

submit an offer 提交报盘

the preference of one's offer 优先报盘

wild speculation 漫天要价

还盘：

acceptable a. 可以接受的，可以使用的

adopt (employ, use) v. 采用（某种价格术语）

average price 平均价格

bargain v. 讨价还价

base price 底价

be equivalent to 相当于

be outbidding 高于……的价

bedrock price 最低价

bid n. & v. 递价，出价，递盘（由买方发出）

buying price 买价

ceiling price 最高价，顶价

CIF ex ship's hold CIF 舱底交货价

CIF liner terms CIF 班轮条件

closing price 收盘价

combined offer 联盘，搭配报盘

concentration of offers 集中报盘

cost and freight（C&F） 成本加运费价，离岸加运费价

cost level 成本费用水平

cost price 成本价

cost, insurance and freight（CIF） 成本加保险费、运费价，到岸价

current price 时价，现价

economically ad. 经济地，便宜地

employ v. 用……计价，采用……

ex dock duty paid 目的港码头完税交货价

ex dock duty unpaid 目的港码头未完税交货价

ex factory 工厂交货价

ex plantation 农场交货价

ex ship 目的港船上交货价

ex warehouse 仓库交货价

exceptional price 特价

exchange rate 汇率

extra price 附加价

FOB liner terms FOB 班轮条件

FOB plane 飞机离岸价（用于紧急情况）

FOB stowed 船上交货并理舱价

FOB trimmed 船上交货并平舱价

FOB under tackle FOB 吊钩下交货价

free alongside ship (FAS) 船边交货价

free on board（FOB） 船上交货价，离岸价

free on rail (FOR) 火车交货价

free on truck (FOT) 汽车交货价

get a bid 得到递价

going price 现价

gross price 毛价

hover v. 徘徊于……，盘旋于……

lump offer 综合报盘（针对两种以上商品）

make a bid 递价

market price 市价

maximum price 最高价

minimum price 最低价

moderate price 公平价格

moderately ad. 适当地，合适地，适度地

net price 净价

new price 新价

nominal price 有行无市的价格

offer letter 报价书

offer list/book 报价单

offer price 售价

offer sheet 出售货物单

offeree n. 被发价人，受盘人

offerer n. 发价人，报盘人

offering date 报价日

offering period 报价有效期限

offeror n. 发价（盘）人

old price 旧价

opening price 开价，开盘价

original price 原价

pass over 转给，转嫁

present price 现价

prevailing price 现价

price n. 价格，定价，开价

price calculation 价格计算

price card 价格目录

price contract 价格合约

price control 价格控制

price current 市价表

price effect 价格效应

price format 价格目录，价格表

price index/price indices 物价指数

price limit 价格限制

price list 定价政策，价格目录，价格单

price of commodities 物价

price of factory 厂价

price per unit 单价

price ratio 比价

price regulation 价格调整

price structure 价格构成

price support 价格支持

price tag 价格标签，标价条

price terms 价格条款

price theory 价格理论

priced *a.* 已标价的，有定价的

priced catalogue 定价目录

pricing *n.* 定价，标价

pricing cost 定价成本

pricing method 定价方法

pricing policy 定价政策

retail price 零售价

rock-bottom *a.* 最低的

rock-bottom price 最低价

ruling price 市价，时价

selling price 卖价

special price 特价

utmost *n.* 极限，竭尽所能

wholesale price 批发价

Unit

3

Acceptance or Conclusion of Business

接受或成交

Learning Resources

Warming-up

In international business, acceptance is indispensable for conclusion of business. It is actually a reserved assent of both the buyer and the seller who are willing to conclude the business in accordance with the terms and conditions agreed upon after many rounds of negotiations. An effective acceptance should have the following qualities or prerequisites. First, an effective acceptance is based upon the buyer's complete acceptance of the firm offer, or upon the seller's confirmation of the buyer's acceptance of a non-firm offer, or upon the seller's acceptance of the buyer's counteroffer. Secondly, an acceptance is effective only when the offer is between the offeror and the offeree. The acceptance of the offer by any third party is not binding upon the offeror. Thirdly, an acceptance is effective only when the acceptance is made within the validity of the offer. Fourthly, even if business is concluded orally, an acceptance of an offer should be confirmed in written form. Fifthly, the acceptance and conclusion of the business must be based upon an agreement freely entered into without any duress or undue influence. Sixthly, the parties concerned must have legal capacity to enter into a contract. Lastly, the acceptance must be something that the law will uphold and treat as binding on both parties.

Dialogues

▶ **Dialogue 1** **Talking over Prices for Plastic Products**

Mr. Larsen (L), an Indian businessman, comes to talk over prices for plastic products with Ms. Peng Yuan (P), Chinese businesswoman of Hyland Light Industrial Products Co.

L: Ms. Peng, I'd appreciate it if you make us an offer for plastic wares, which should be microwave- and refrigerator-safe.

P: I'd be glad to. The commodities you just mentioned fall in with our business scope. I wonder what specifications you would like to order.

L: We need wares with a capacity of one cup, two cups, three cups and all the way up to seven cups. What is the price for this 7-piece set?

P: We offer at US$13.40 per set, CIF Bombay, usual terms.

L: We have been thinking to purchase at around 12.5 dollars per set. Do you think you are able to come down to this level?

P: I'm sorry. We can't agree to your price. However, to regular customers we can give a 40 cents discount. 13 dollars is our bottom price. I think it's necessary to point out that our plastic wares won't do any harm to people's health. They can stand a temperature of as low as minus 30℃ and as high as 200℃.

L: OK, I think I'll accept 13 dollars. As for the other terms we'll just do as usual.

P: Great.

▶ Dialogue 2   Negotiating the Rice Price

Mr. Xiang Long (X), manager of Northeast Foodstuffs Imp. & Exp. Corporation, is negotiating with a Polish businessman, Mr. Gallon (G), over the rice price.

G: Mr. Xiang, we have discussed your offer for 5,000 metric tons of rice. We think your price is on the high side. The other day I gave you our counter-offer. Have you considered it?

X: Your counter-offer at RMB2,500 per metric ton. We did discuss it, but we think this price really leaves us no margin. Do you think RMB2,900 is acceptable? Offering this, we already give up most of our profit.

G: What about if we meet half way to make a deal at RMB2,700? We think this price is quite reasonable and about the same as the world market level.

X: OK, deal! We'll sell you 5,000 metric tons of rice of Northeast China at RMB2,700 per metric ton CIF European Main Ports.

G: Sounds great. Could you manage to ship the goods by June 15?

X: Yes, we can, if you open the L/C no later than May 15.

G: All right. I'm glad we agreed upon the price. I believe the success of this deal will be a great step forward in our relationship.

X: So do I.

▶ Dialogue 3 Negotiating the Terms and Conditions of a Contract

Mr. Zhao (Z), from Tianjin Machinery Import & Export Corporation, has secured an order from an American importer for his corporation's garden tools. He is now negotiating the terms of the contract with Ms. Jackson (J) from the importing company.

Z: Well, Ms. Jackson. It seems to me that we've come quite a long way, but there are still a few points left over to clear up.

J: Yes, let's go over the terms and conditions of the contract. If you have any comments about them, do not hesitate to say so.

Z: Good, now the price for 1,000 sets of garden tools, quality and design as shown in our catalogue at USD6.50 each set CIF New York. So the business is closed at this price.

J: Yes, that's right. As to packing, we hope you pack the goods in wooden cases.

Z: Oh, Ms. Jackson. As I told you before, cartons are as seaworthy as wooden cases and even have more advantages over the latter. For instance, they are easier to handle and cheaper in cost. We've never received any complaint about it from our clients. You can take it from me that they are strong enough to stand rough handling.

J: All right, cartons then. Well, the shipment I understand is to be made before December, isn't it? We can't accept any delay.

Z: Yes. Rest assured that shipment will be effected according to the contract stipulations. But if my memory serves me, "Transshipment via Hong Kong allowed" is what we agreed upon, isn't it?

J: Ah, yes, I remember. Now, how about the terms of payment?

Z: Payment is to be made by irrevocable L/C at 60 days sight to be opened 5 to 20 days prior to the date of delivery.

J: I wonder whether you would consider 90 days' L/C as I suggested. I sincerely hope you are able to make a last minute change on this aspect.

Z: Sorry. That's impossible. As I said, 60 days is the result of great concession made on our part. I think we'd better keep it to what has been agreed upon.

J: Well, I guess there is no way out. I'll see about the opening of the L/C as soon as I get home.

Z: Thanks. The next point is insurance. I'm sure you are quite familiar with our usual terms.

If you have no objection, let's take it as agreed.

J: No objection at all. I remember it is to be covered by the seller for 110% of the invoice value against all risks and war risk.

Z: Right, Ms. Jackson. Anything else you would like to discuss?

J: OK. There is the last thing to make clear. How do we resolve the case where both parties hold different opinions on the standard of the goods?

Z: Oh, suppose we have a dispute, we can resolve the case by submitting the dispute to arbitration by the Chinese International Trade Arbitration Commission.

J: All right. I'm glad that our discussion has come to a successful conclusion. Are we anywhere near a contract yet? I hope we can sign it very soon.

Z: I'll contact you as soon as the formal contract is ready.

J: Thank you.

▶ Dialogue 4   Finalizing a Contract

Now Mr. Zhao (Z) and Ms. Jackson (J) are taking one more look before signing the contract.

Z: Now, we've finally reached an agreement on the problems that need to be worked out. Shall we sign the contract now?

J: Just a minute. Generally speaking, a contract cannot be changed after both parties have signed it. So we'd better make sure one more time that we've got them right.

Z: That's a good idea.

J: First of all, about the format of our contract. There are two of the originals of the contract, both in Chinese and English. So they are equally authentic in terms of law. Here's a copy for you to check.

Z: Thank you. I have no objection. It contains all we have agreed upon during our negotiations. To make sure no important items have been overlooked, let's check all the terms listed in the contract and see if there is anything not in conformity with the terms we agreed on.

J: OK, let's start from the name of the commodity, specifications, quantity, unit piece... well, it looks good enough to me. You've done a good job.

Z: Thank you. Since your company enjoys a good reputation, we want to make sure we keep your business.

J: We always think our commercial reputation is of primary importance, and promise that the execution of the contract will not be compromised, no matter what happens.

Z: It's really nice to get to know all of you. Shall we sign the contract now?

J: Yes, I'm looking forward to this moment.

(After signing the contract)

Z: Let's propose a toast to the success of the negotiations and to our future cooperation. Cheers!

J: Cheers! Let's congratulate ourselves on having brought this transaction to a successful conclusion.

Words and Expressions

indispensable *a.* 必不可少的，必需的	uphold *v.* 维护，支持
reserved *a.* 有保留的，有条件的	treat as 作为……看待
assent *n.* 同意，赞成	plastic wares 塑料器具，塑料制品
in accordance with 依照，按照	microwave *n.* 微波炉
effective *a.* 有效的	fall in with 与……巧合，与……相称
prerequisite *n.* 先决条件，前提，必备条件	business scope 经营范围，业务范围
be based upon 以……为基础，以……为条件	capacity *n.* 容量
	7-piece set 7件一套，7件套
confirmation *n.* 确认	usual terms 普通条件，正常条件
third party 第三方	minus *a.* 零下的
in written form 用书面形式	on the high side 偏高
enter into 签订，缔约	margin *n.* 利润边际
duress *n.* 强迫，威胁	meet half way 各让一半
undue *a.* 不适当的，不正当的	make a deal 达成交易
legal capacity 法律能力	European main ports 欧洲主要港口
	rest assured that... 尽管放心……

Notes

1. 接受

在进出口贸易中，洽谈交易程序一般是按"询盘—发盘—还盘—接受—签订合同"这五个环节来进行的。接受是达成交易和订立合同必不可少的环节。接受在法律上叫作承诺。它是指受盘人在发盘有效期内完全同意发盘的全部内容，愿意订立合同的一种表示。一项有效的接受一般必须具备以下条件。

（1）必须是受盘人对一项实盘的完全同意。

（2）必须是发盘所规定的受盘人表示同意才有效。

（3）必须是受盘人在发盘有效期内或合理时间内表示同意才有效。

（4）接受应由受盘人做出声明或以其他行为方式表示，并且这种表示传达给发盘人后才开始有效。

2. 成交

FOB（free on board），即装运港船上交货价，是指卖方在约定的装运港将货物交到买方指定的船上。按此术语成交，卖方负责办理出口手续，买方负责派船接运货物，买卖双方费用和风险的划分以装运港船舷为界。

CFR（cost and freight），即成本加运费价，是指卖方必须负担货物运至约定目的港所需的成本和运费。

CIF（cost, insurance and freight），即成本加保险费加运费。按此价格术语成交，货价构成因素中包括从转运港至约定的目的港通常的运费和约定的保险费，即卖方除具有与 CFR 术语相同的义务外，还应为买方办理保险并支付保险费。

3. The commodities you just mentioned fall in with our business scope.

您刚才说的这些商品都在我们的业务范围之内。

4. …this price really leaves us no margin.

……这个价格没给我们留下任何利润。

5. What about we meet half way to make a deal at RMB2,700?

我们各让一半以 2 700 元成交怎么样？

6. if my memory serves me   如果我没有记错的话

7. If you have no objection, let's take it as agreed.

如果你没有反对意见，我们就把它定下来。

8. all risks and war risk   一切险和战争险

9. … we can resolve the case by submitting the dispute to arbitration by the Chinese International Trade Arbitration Commission.

……我们可以通过把争议呈给中国国际贸易仲裁委员会的方式来解决。

10. … your company enjoys a good reputation …

……贵公司享有很好的声誉……

Useful Sentences

1. Our price is quite reasonable and other buyers in your market have accepted it.
   我们的价格很合理，而且已经为你们市场的其他买主所接受了。

2. Please accept our offer and confirm the above-mentioned terms immediately.
   请即接受我方报盘，并尽快确认以上条款。

3. Owing to heavy commitments, we can not accept fresh business at present.
   由于订货太多，目前我们无法接受新的业务。

4. Taking the quality into consideration, we accept your offer.
   考虑到质量，我们接受你方报盘。

5. We are pleased to have transacted our first act of business with your firm.
   我们很高兴同贵公司达成了首批交易。

6. We have succeeded in putting through the deal of five hundred bicycles.
   我们成功地达成了500辆自行车的交易。

7. We have faxed our confirmation of your order and you are requested to open the L/C as soon as possible.
   我们已发传真确认接受你方订单，请你们尽快开立信用证。

8. We strongly recommend acceptance as our stocks are running low.
   由于存货日渐趋少，我们力荐贵方接受我方报盘。

9. With an eye to future business, we'll accept payment by D/P this time.
   为了今后的业务，我们这次可以接受付款交单方式。

10. We are sorry that we cannot accept your counteroffer, as the price quoted by us is quite realistic.
    报给你方的价格已经很实际，很抱歉我方不能接受你方还盘。

11. The price you quoted being found workable, we have faxed you our acceptance.
    我们认为你们所报价格可行，已发传真给你方表示接受。

12. We accept your offer provided that shipment is made in November.
    如能在11月份装船，我们就接受你方报价。

13. Although the prevailing quotations are somewhat higher, we will accept the order on the same terms as before with the view of encouraging business.
    尽管目前报价有些偏高，但为了促进今后业务的开展，我们仍将按过去条件接受你方订单。

14. Here is our contract. Would you please read it again?

这是我们的合同，请你再仔细地看看好吗？

15. We will have the contract ready for signature.
    我们会准备好待签合同的。

16. Do you have any comment to make about this clause?
    你对该条款还有什么意见吗？

17. Don't you think we should add this sentence here?
    难道你不认为我们应该在此增加这句话吗？

18. If one side fails to honor the contract, the other side is entitled to cancel it.
    如果一方不履行合同，另一方有权撤销合同。

19. Please check all the terms listed in the contract and see if there is anything not in conformity with the terms we agreed on.
    请认真核对一下合同中的各项条款，以确定与我们当初所谈好的各项内容是否相符。

20. I agree to the terms concerning the packing and shipping marks.
    我同意关于包装和唛头的条款。

21. We hope to be able to sign the contract by next Monday.
    我们希望下周一能够签订合同。

22. We both want to sign a contract, and we have to make some concessions to do it.
    我们双方都想签订这个合同，所以我们都得做出让步才行。

23. Our current contract is about to expire, and we'll need to discuss a new one.
    我们手上的合同马上就到期了，我们得重新拟定一份才行。

24. We ought to clear up problems arising from the old contract.
    我们得解决先前那个合同带来的问题。

Exercises

I **Translate the following sentences orally.**

A. **From Chinese to English**

1. 在签订这份合同前，让我们再来核对一下条款。

2. 我又仔细地看了一下合同，发现需要补充一项条款。

3. 在我们达成最终协议之前，还有两个问题需要澄清一下。

4. 你不觉得应该仔细检查一下合同，以免遗漏什么吗？

5. 假如谈判不能解决问题，双方同意将争议交由双方都能接受的第三方仲裁。

B. From English to Chinese

1. We can't agree with the alterations and amendments to the contract.

2. If possible, I would like to bend the rules a little. But in terms of payment, we can only accept the irrevocable L/C.

3. We are really glad to see you are so constructive in helping settle the problems regarding the signing of the contract.

4. Any dispute arising out of the contract shall be settled through friendly negotiation.

5. We should make it clear that no matter which party cannot honor the contract, the other party is entitled to claim for losses.

Ⅱ Situational practice.

Make dialogues according to the following situations.

1. Mr. Boney, an Italian importer, discusses with you an offer on 6,000 sets of cooking utensils. Having bargained for some time, he accepts your revised price. After going over the payment and other general terms, the business is concluded. Both you and Mr. Boney take one more look before signing the contract.

2. You are the sales manager representing Huabei Heavy-duty Machinery Imp. & Exp. Corp. A businessman from Thailand has ordered a total of USD500,000 worth of your heavy-duty machinery equipment. The contract was drafted by the Thai company. You find one provision should be added: the insurance premium should be borne by the Thai party since the price is determined on a CFR basis.

对话汉译

对话 1   磋商塑料制品的价格

印度客商拉尔森先生（L）前来与汉兰达轻工产品公司的中方业务员彭媛女士（P）磋商塑料制品的价格问题。

L: 彭女士，我们需要能用于微波炉和电冰箱的那种塑料品。如您能给我们发盘，我们将不胜感激。

P: 我很高兴给你发盘。您刚才说的这些商品都在我们的业务范围内。不知道你想要哪种规格的？

L: 我们需要容量是一杯、两杯、三杯直到七杯的容器。这种 7 件一套的需要多少钱？

P: 我们报价每套 13 美元 40 美分，孟买到岸价，常规条款。

L: 我们一直在想以每套大约 12.5 美元的价格购买。你们能降到这个水平吗？

P: 很抱歉，我们不能这样做。但是对于老客户，我们可以给予 40 美分的折扣。13 美元是我们的最低价。我认为有必要指出的是，我们的塑料制品不会对健康有害。它们可以承受低达零下 30 摄氏度和高达 200 摄氏度的温度。

L: 好吧，我想我接受 13 美元了。至于其他条款，我们就按往常那么处理。

P: 好极了。

▶ 对话 2 磋商大米价格

东北粮食进出口公司经理向龙先生（X）正在与波兰客商加伦先生（G）磋商大米的价格问题。

G: 向先生，我们已经讨论了你们关于 5 000 公吨大米的发盘。我们认为你们的价格过高。那天我们已经给你还盘了。你们考虑了吗？

X: 你们的还盘是每公吨 2 500 元。我们讨论过，但是认为你们的价格没给我们留下任何利润。你认为 2 900 元能接受吗？这么做，我们已经放弃了大部分利润。

G: 我们各让一半以 2 700 元成交怎么样？我们认为这个价格是合理的，与国际市场行情很接近。

X: 好的，成交！我们就按每公吨 2 700 元的欧洲主要港口到岸价向你方出售 5 000 公吨中国东北大米。

G: 好极了。你们能在 6 月 15 日前装运吗？

X: 如果你们能于 5 月 15 日前开立信用证，我们就可以装运。

G: 那好的。我很高兴我们能够就价格达成一致。我相信这笔交易的成功会使我们的关系向前迈出一大步。

X: 我也是这么认为的。

▶ 对话 3 就合同条款进行磋商

来自天津机械进出口公司的赵先生（Z）收到一位美国进口商对其公司园艺工具的订单。他正在和来自美方进口公司的杰克逊夫人（J）商谈合同条款。

Z: 好的，杰克逊夫人。我们大概已经谈得差不多了，但是还有一些需要我们明确的地方。

J: 是的，那就让我们来看看这个合同的条款和条件吧。你如果对其有任何的解释说明，就尽管说。

Z: 好的。这 1 000 套园艺工具就按照我方产品目录里面的价格、质量和样式向贵方供货。每套到达纽约的 CIF 价格为 6.50 美元。因此，我们这笔生意就按这个价格成交。

J: 好的。至于货物的包装，我们希望贵方使用木箱子包装。

Z: 哦，杰克逊夫人。正如我以前和你说的那样，纸箱包装与木箱包装一样适应海运，而且比起木箱包装来更加具有优势。比如说，搬运更加方便且成本花费更低。而且我们从来没有收到顾客对纸箱包装的投诉。我敢保证纸箱包装同样能够经得起搬运。

J: 那好吧，就用纸箱包装吧。哦，对了，据我所知，货物航运是在 12 月份以前出发，对吧？我们可耽搁不起啊！

Z: 是的，你尽管放心。我们一定会按照合同约定给你们发货。如果我没有记错的话，我们当初是不是谈好"允许在香港转船"？

J: 啊，是的！我记着呢！那么，支付方式呢？

Z: 使用期限为 60 天的不可撤销信用证支付，且于交货前 5 至 20 天开立。

J: 贵方可否考虑使用按照我当初提出的期限为 90 天的不可撤销信用证？我真诚地希望贵方能最后在这方面做出调整。

Z: 对不起，这个恐怕做不到。正如我所说，60 天期限是我方能做出的最大让步。我想我们双方应该严格按照当初我们商定的办理。

J: 那好吧，除此之外，也没有其他的办法了。我一回去就马上开立信用证。

Z: 谢谢你的理解！接下来，我们谈谈关于保险的事。我想你肯定非常熟悉我们的惯例。如果你没有反对意见，我们就把它定下来。

J: 我完全接受。我记得由卖方按发票面值的 1.1 倍支付一切险和战争险费用。

Z: 对的，杰克逊夫人。你还有什么需要我们双方共同商讨的吗？

J: 好的，还有最后一件需要明确的事。如果我们双方在货物标准上存在争议的话，怎样解决？

Z: 哦，那好办。假设我们双方存在争议。我们可以通过把争议呈给中国国际贸易仲裁委员会的方式来解决。

J: 好的。我很高兴我们的商谈终于促成了这笔生意。那么，我们可以签订合同了吗？我希望能够尽快签订。

Z: 我们一旦准备好正式的合同就立即通知你。

J: 谢谢！

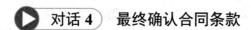

对话 4 最终确认合同条款

在签订正式合同之前，赵先生（Z）和杰克逊夫人（J）进一步核实了合同条款。

Z: 现在我们双方已经在需要明确解决的问题上达成了一致。可以签合同了吗？

J: 等一下。一般来说，一旦双方签字确认后，合同就不能更改了。因此，我认为我们最好还是再看一看我们在各方面是否都达成了一致。

Z: 好主意！

J: 首先是关于合同的格式。原版合同中英文各一份，它们在法律上具有同等效力，这一份你拿去看看。

Z: 谢谢，我完全同意。它包括了我们在前期商谈中达成的所有条款。为了确保没有遗漏重要内容，让我们再认真地看一看合同中所列出的所有条款，看是否符合我们当初商定的条款。

J: 好的，那就让我们从商品名称、规格、数量、件数开始吧。哦，看起来很好。你干得真不错！

Z: 谢谢。因为贵公司享有很好的声誉，我们想保持与你们的生意来往。

J: 我们一直把商业信誉放在首位，并郑重承诺，无论发生什么事情，我们都得严格履行合同。

Z: 很高兴你让我对贵方有了一个真正的了解。我们现在可以签合同了吧？

J: 好啊，我可一直都期望这一时刻的到来！

（合同签订后）

Z: 来吧，我提议为我们这一次合同的成功签订和我们将来的合作干杯！

J: 好吧，让我们为这次生意的最后成交而干杯！

Extended Reading

Acceptance

Acceptance is an indispensable link in concluding a deal and signing a contract. It is stipulated in the laws of some countries that only offer and acceptance are the two required elements, failure of which will result in no contract. An acceptance or a confirmation is in fact an unreserved assent of the buyers or the sellers, who after mutual negotiations are willing to enter into a contract in accordance with terms and conditions agreed upon. A deal is concluded when the seller's firm offer is accepted by the buyers or a non-firm offer, after being accepted by the buyers, is confirmed by the sellers. In cases where the buyers have made a counter-offer, or taken the initiative by placing a firm order or a firm bid with the sellers, containing all necessary terms and conditions, the seller's acceptance concludes the deal. In a word, only after the exchanging of a number of letters, cables or telexes or faxes can the two parties reach a consensus on all terms. In such a case the buyers, when finally placing a formal order, would confirm the terms and conditions, agreed upon for the sellers' acceptance. In light of usual practice in foreign trade, an acceptance should abide by the following requirements.

An acceptance must be absolute and unconditional. It should be an unreserved assent to all the terms put forward in the offer. In principle, if any additions, modifications or limitations to the offer are made, they are a counter-offer, and not an acceptance.

An acceptance can be made by an act performed by an offeree, such as one relating to the dispatch of the goods or payment of the price. In this way, the offeree may indicate assent without notice to the offeror. The acceptance is effective at the moment the act is performed, provided that the act is performed within the stipulated period of time.

An acceptance must be clearly expressed by the offeree's verbal or written statement. Silence or inactivity is by no means an acceptance.

An acceptance must be made by the offeree within the valid period of a firm offer. As a rule, an acceptance goes into effect immediately as soon as it reaches the offeror. However, the laws of some countries stipulate that an acceptance begins to function the moment the letter or cable of acceptance is posted or dispatched. A contract is thus concluded at this very moment in spite of the fact that the letter of cable is likely to be lost in the mail or transmission. To avoid subsequent disputes or confusion in this respect, it is the practice to clarify to the offeree that an acceptance would not be valid unless the letter or cable is received before the time limit.

Topic discussion:

1. What is the importance of acceptance?
2. How do you make your acceptance more effective?

其他常用词汇和短语

advance shipment　提前装运
commitments　*n.*　所承诺的事
confirm one's order　确认订单
entertain　*v.*　准备考虑
execute an order　执行订单
expedite shipment　加速装运

extend shipment　延期装运
favor　*v.*　有利于
in sb's favor　以……为受益人
lodge　*v.*　提出（报告、抗议、申诉等），
　　　正式提出
make/effect shipment　装运

more or less 或多或少，大约，……左右	rest assured 放心
	shipping/shipment advice 装船通知
optional port 选择性港口	sign a treaty 签订条约
port of destination 目的港	sign and return a copy of... for one's file
port of shipment 装运港	签退一份……以供某人存档
repeat order 续订订单	terms of payment 付款条件

Unit

4

Credit Inquiry

资信调查

Learning Resources

Warming-up

What is credit inquiry? In international business, credit inquiry is made by traders requesting the financial position, credit, reputation, and business methods of other firms. Before a firm starts business with a new customer or company, it is the usual practice to make credit inquiry so as to obtain all the information possible about the firm one is going to enter into business relations with, to well protect oneself in case any disputes arise, and to safeguard the interests of both parties involved. So credit inquiry is of the utmost importance. It is vital to the future cooperation of the traders.

There are various ways of obtaining credit information, for instance, banks, chambers of commerce, inquiry agencies, or business connections. The information obtained from a bank or from a chamber of commerce is generally reliable and free of charge. However, a bank will not give information directly to an unknown inquirer unless the inquiry comes from one of its fellow banks. Therefore, when taking up a bank reference, the trader had better apply to his own bank for credit inquiry. From the inquiry agency the inquirer can also get the needed information but such information should be paid off. Besides, the inquirer can also refer to other sources such as business partners who are likely to provide the information required.

Dialogues

▶ Dialogue 1   Seeking for a Credit Inquiry

Before entering into a contract with NHK Trading Company in Japan, Mr. Shang (S) goes to his bank to seek for credit inquiry. The following is the conversation between him and the bank clerk (C).

C: Good morning, Mr. Shang. What can I do for you?

S: Well, we have got a new partner in a big transaction, and planned to sign a contract at the

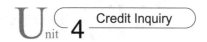

end of this month. So I'd like to know more about that company.

C: You mean you want us to make a status inquiry?

S: Yes, I want to get the credit information about our cooperative partner.

C: Which country is that company registered in?

S: In Japan. Will it be difficult?

C: No, it's not complicated. The only thing for you to do is to fill in a form and sign it. Then we will send it to our branch office or agent in Japan by the fastest way. They will do as your request, and then send the report back. Of course it is done in a confidential way, and we hope you will keep it confidential.

S: Yes, of course we will. Well, what about the service fee?

C: For long-term clients we charge only direct fees like telephone or fax fee.

S: May I take the form back and fill it?

C: Yes, of course. Please call me any time if you have any question.

▶ Dialogue 2　A Good Report on the Credit Inquiry

About one week ago, Sydney Trading Company asked their banker for credit inquiry on a foreign trading company. Now there is the credit report. The following is the conversation between the bank clerk (C) and Mr. Keddy (K) of Sydney Trading Company.

C: Hello, this is Consultant Department of Bank of China, Beijing Branch.

K: Is there the status report about Imperial Trading Co.?

C: Yes. We have just completed our inquiries concerning the firm mentioned in your trust form.

K: Any troubles?

C: No, this is a favorable reply. It's a private firm and enjoys good reputation in its area. As the credit report shows, it's always punctual to meet its commitments. It seems to be safe to do business with them.

K: Great. Now we can do business with them with assurance.

C: Besides, according to the report, the technique of this company is among the best in the world. We have no doubt about their technique.

K: Thank you for your information.

C: Mr. Keddy, this information is of course supplied in the strictest confidence.

K: Uh, yes, we can assure you that any information you give us will be treated in absolute confidence.

C: When will you come back and take the written report?

K: Right now. I'll come shortly.

▶ Dialogue 3 A Dissatisfactory Report on the Credit Inquiry

About one week ago, Sydney Trading Company asked their banker for credit inquiry on a foreign trading company. Now there is the credit report. The following is the conversation between the bank clerk (C) and Mr. Keddy (K) of Sydney Trading Company.

C: Hello, this is Consultant Department of Bank of China, Beijing Branch.

K: Is there the status report about Imperial Trading Co.?

C: Yes. We have just completed our inquiries concerning the firm you mentioned in your trust form.

K: Any troubles?

C: Our records show that some of their accounts have been outstanding for long periods. Recent difficulties that seem to be due to bad management have resulted in considerable borrowing at a high rate of interest.

K: What a pity!

C: We are regretting to inform you of it. Another company's experience with them has not been satisfactory. It is a condition of this letter that the name of this company will not be disclosed in the event of our report being passed on to your client.

K: No problem. Any information you may give us will be treated as strictly confidential and expenses accruing from this inquiry will be gladly paid by us upon receipt of your bill.

▶ Dialogue 4 Asking Customers for Credit Information

Bank of China asked Sydney Trading Company for credit information.

B: Hello, is that Candy of Sydney Trading Company?

C: Yes, this is. Who is that?

B: This is Consultant Department of Bank of China, Beijing Branch.

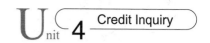

C: Yeah, what is up?

B: As you know, in our line of work, we depend on good reports about our projects to win further business. Our clients always shop around and look for references before committing themselves. We would like to use your company as a reference when we discuss similar affairs in the same occasion. Would you agree to our suggestion that future clients should call you?

C: Sure! We are willing to offer our help.

B: It is so kind of you. Thank you a lot.

Words and Expressions

transaction *n.* 交易	status report 资信报告
status inquiry 信用状况调查，资信调查	trust form 委托表
credit information 信用信息	punctual *a.* 准时的
cooperative partner 合作伙伴	meet one's commitment 履行义务
register *v.* 登记，注册	assurance *n.* 有把握，放心
complicated *a.* 复杂的	in strict confidence 严格保密
branch office 分支机构，分公司	assure *v.* 向……保证
confidential *a.* 保密的	shortly *ad.* 立即，马上
service fee 服务费	incur *v.* 遭受
direct fee 直接费用	

Notes

1. 关于资信调查

1）资信调查概述

资信调查是企业信用管理的基础。通过资信调查，企业能够及时、系统、客观地了解和掌握客户的资信状况，并以此作为企业进行信用销售是否授信或授信多少的重要依据。其具有真实性、综合性、前瞻性、合作性、机密性、差别性的特点。

2）对客户资信调查的内容和范围

（1）国外企业的组织机构情况，包括企业的性质、创建历史、内部组织机构、主要负责人及担任的职务、分支机构等。调查中，应弄清厂商企业的中英文名称、详细地址，防止出现差错。

（2）政治情况，主要指企业负责人的政治背景，与政界的关系及对我国的政治态度等。

（3）资信情况，包括企业的资金和信用这两个方面。资金是指企业的注册资本、财产及资产负债情况等；信用是指企业的经营作风、履约信誉等。这是客户资信调查的主要内容，特别是对中间商更应重视。例如，有的客户愿和我们洽谈上亿美元的投资项目，但经调查其注册资本只有几十万美元。对这样的客户，我们就该打上个问号。

（4）经营范围，主要是指企业生产或经营的商品、经营的性质，是代理商、生产商，还是零售批发商等。

（5）经营能力，每年的营业额、销售渠道、经营方式及在当地和国际市场上的贸易关系等。

此外，对客户资信进行调查后，应建立档案卡备查，并分类建立客户档案。总之，要善于利用不同类型客户的长处，为我服务。

3）资信调查的途径

（1）通过银行调查，这是一种常见的方法，按国际习惯，调查客户的情况属于银行的业务范围；在我国，一般委托中国银行办理。向银行查询客户资信，一般不收费或少量收费。

（2）通过国外的工商团体进行调查，如商会、同业公会、贸易协会等，一般都接受国外厂商委托调查所在地企业的情况。但通过这种渠道得来的资信，要经过认真分析，不能轻信。

（3）通过我国驻外机构和在实际业务活动中对客户进行考察所得的材料，一般比较具体可靠，对业务的开展有较大的参考价值。此外，外国出版的企业名录、厂商年鉴及其他有关资料，对了解客户的经营范围和活动情况也有一定的参考价值。

4）资信调查报告

解读资信报告需关注以下几个要点。

（1）开业时间。经营历史长的企业，尤其是经历过经济危机的企业，一般而言意味着拥有较强的生存能力。对于开业时间短于一年、注册资本小且无任何经营和财务信息的新买方，企业与其交易时要格外小心。

（2）资本相关信息。多数报告中的资本信息包含有注册资本、实付资本及资本历史变更情况。注册资本及实付资本的金额及两者的比例在一定程度上可反映出目标公司自身的规模。关于资本变更、大幅增资的信息可在很大程度上反映出目标公司在资本变更时业务扩张的强烈愿望及对未来发展正面积极的预期。

（3）雇员人数与经营地信息。考察企业的规模实力，经营地和雇员人数是相对比较稳定可靠的信息。统计分析表明，人均经营地面积与企业信用状况之间存在一定程度的

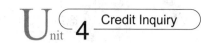

正向联系，雇员规模也是反映公司实力的重要指标。

最后，专家建议，在利用资信报告评估买方信用时，一方面需对现有资料进行据实评价；另一方面，要在尊重事实的基础上合理质疑，对发现的问题善于思考和追究，并设法积极求证。

2. I want to get the credit information about our cooperative partner.

我想得到合作伙伴的信用信息。

3. Of course it is done in a confidential way, and we hope you will keep it confidential.

当然了，这是在保密状态下进行的，我们也希望你们保密。

Useful Sentences

1. Please accept our thanks for the trouble you have taken.

有劳贵方，不胜感激。

2. We are obliged to thank you for your kind attention to this matter.

不胜感激贵方对此事的关照。

3. We tender you our sincere thanks for your generous treatment of us in this affair.

对贵方在此事中的慷慨之举，深表感谢。

4. Allow us to thank you for the kindness extended to us.

对贵方之盛情，不胜感谢。

5. We thank you for the special care you have given to the matter.

贵方对此悉心关照，不胜感激。

6. We should be grateful for your furnishing us details of your requirements.

如承赐示具体要求，不胜感激。

7. We assure you of our best services at all times.

我方保证向贵方随时提供最佳服务。

8. If there is anything we can do to help you, we shall be more than pleased to do so.

贵公司若有所需求，我公司定尽力效劳。

9. It would give us a great pleasure to render you a similar service should an opportunity occur.

我方如有机会同样效劳贵方，将不胜欣慰。

10. We spare no efforts in endeavoring to be of service to you.

我方将不遗余力为贵方效劳。

11. We shall be very glad to handle for you at very low commission charges.

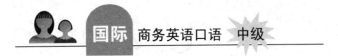

我方很乐意受理此事，而且收费低廉。

12. We take this opportunity to re-emphasize that we shall, at all times, do everything possible to give you whatever information you desire.

我们借此机会再次强调，定会尽力随时提供贵方所需的信息。

13. We solicit a continuance of your confidence and support.

恳请贵方继续给予信任和大力支持。

xercises

I **Complete the following dialogues.**

1. **A:** _____?

（贵行能为我公司做个资信调查吗？）

   B: Of course. We have a special department dealing with credit inquiry.

2. **A:** What kind of services do you offer?

   B: _____

   _____.

（我行向客户提供各种咨询服务，比如贸易调查、财务咨询等，以及您所提及的资信调查。）

3. **A:** That's great. Well, we have got a new partner in a big transaction and plan to sign a contract next month. _____.

（因此，我们想了解一些那家公司的资信情况。）

   B: OK. No problem.

4. **A:** What do you want to know about this American company?

   B: _____.

（我们想知道该公司还款能力方面的情况。）

5. **A:** When shall we have the credit report?

   B: You know, it is in a confidential way. _____.

（我们将尽快把资信调查报告交给你们。）

II **Situational practice.**

Make dialogues according to the following situations.

1. Suppose you are Mr. Rong, the General Manager of Guangdong Import & Export Co., Ltd.

70

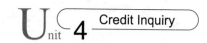

Your company is going to do business with a Thai company. The final contract is due to be signed at the end of next month. Now you come to the Consultant Department of Bank of China, Guangzhou Branch to ask for a credit inquiry.

2. Suppose you are Ms. Xue, the business manager of North China Domestic Appliances Import & Export Co., Ltd. Your corporation wants to import some appliances from the US-based manufacturer, Consent Domestic Appliances, but you don't know much about it. Now you come to Forester Consultancy to ask them to help you.

对话汉译

▶ **对话 1**   申请资信调查

在与日本的 NHK 贸易公司签约之前，尚先生（S）来到其开户的银行，寻求资信调查信息。下面就是他和银行职员（C）之间的对话。

C: 早上好，先生，有事吗？

S: 是这样的，我们与一位新的贸易伙伴要做一笔大买卖，并计划在月底签约，因此我想更多地了解这家公司。

C: 您的意思是想让我们为你们做个资信调查？

S: 是的，我想得到合作伙伴的信用信息。

C: 这家公司是在哪个国家注册的？

S: 在日本。这很难吗？

C: 不，这并不复杂，您唯一要做的就是填张表并签上您的名字。我们将以最快的速度将表传给日本的分支机构或代办处，他们将依据您的要求办理，然后将报告送回。当然这是在保密状态下进行的，我们也希望你们保密。

S: 我们当然会保密的。那么，要付多少手续费呢？

C: 对长期客户，我们只收电话或传真等直接费用。

S: 我可以把表带回去填吗？

C: 当然可以。如有问题，请随时打电话。

▶ **对话 2**   有利的资信调查报告

大约一周前，悉尼贸易公司要求其开户银行调查一家外国贸易公司的资信情况。目

前，资信报告已到达。下面就是银行职员（C）与悉尼贸易公司的凯迪先生（K）的对话。

C: 您好！这里是中国银行北京分行咨询部。

K: 是关于帝国贸易公司资信报告的消息吗？

C: 是的，我们刚刚完成你们委托表中提到的公司的资信调查。

K: 有什么问题吗？

C: 没有，是一个有利的答复。这是一家私人企业，在本地享有良好的声誉。资信报告显示，他们总是能及时履行义务。看来和他们做生意应该是安全的。

K: 太好了！现在我们可以放心地同他们做生意了。

C: 另外，据调查，这家公司的技术水平是世界一流的。我们毫不怀疑该公司的技术水平。

K: 谢谢您所提供的信息。

C: 凯迪先生，这个信息可要严格保密啊。

K: 嗯，是的，我们保证对你们提供的信息绝对保密。

C: 那您什么时间来拿书面报告呢？

K: 现在，我马上就到。

▶ 对话 3 不利的资信调查报告

大约一周前，悉尼贸易公司要求其开户银行调查一家外国贸易公司的资信情况。目前，资信报告现已到达。下面就是银行职员（C）与悉尼贸易公司的凯迪先生（K）的对话。

C: 喂，我是中国银行北京分行咨询部。

K: 是关于帝国贸易公司的资信报告吗？

C: 我们刚刚完成你们委托表中提到的公司的资信调查。

K: 有什么麻烦吗？

C: 我方资料表明，他们的一些账款长期未曾结清。最近一段时间，也许是因为经营不善所带来的困难，公司借入了大量高利率资金。

K: 太遗憾了！

C: 我方不得不告诉你们，其他公司与他们打交道的经历并不令人满意。本函有一个条件，即在把我方的报告转告贵方的客户时，请勿泄露我行的名称。

K: 没问题！贵公司提供的所有资料，我方将严格保密，所有费用在接到贵公司账单后立即由我公司支付。

▶ 对话 4 请求客户提供资信资料

中国银行请求其客户悉尼贸易公司提供资信资料。

B: 喂，请问是悉尼贸易公司的坎迪吗？

C: 是的，请问你是？

B: 这里是中国银行北京分行咨询部。

C: 哦，请问有什么事情吗？

B: 如您所知，我们的工作是以良好的业务反馈来赢得更多的业务，我们的客户在决定合作之前总是要寻找参考进行一些对比。我们想以贵公司作为参考，可以的话我们的客户会电联贵公司，你们是否同意我们的想法呢？

C: 没问题！我们愿意提供帮助。

B: 太好了，非常感谢！

Extended Reading

1. 咨询函

Dear Sirs,

The under-mentioned firm has recently asked if they could represent us in the marketing of our products in the United States as our sole agent:

Friendship International Trade Co., Ltd.

250 Royal Road

New York, NY 30786

We would be very grateful if you could let us have some information about the financial and business standing of the above firm.

Any information that you may give would be treated in strict confidence and we await your early reply.

Yours faithfully

(Signature)

General Manager

2. 向银行查询新客户资信情况

Dear Sirs,

We have received an order for US$56,500 worth of goods from Atlantic Electronic Co., Ltd., USA. They have given us your bank as a reference. We wish to know if they are good for this amount and in every way trustworthy and reliable. We shall be most grateful for any information you give us.

We should of course treat any advice you tell us in strict confidence and be pleased to perform the similar service for you in the future. We enclose a stamped and addressed envelope for your reply.

Yours faithfully,

(Signature)

3. 向客户查询信用及经营情况

Dear Sirs,

We will be obliged if you will kindly give us the information about the credit standing of Watson & Jones Newcastle International Trade Co., Ltd. in your city. We understand that you have regular transactions with the firm. So we take the liberty to ask you to give your views concerning the actual position of the firm in order that we may take steps to avoid getting into trouble.

Any information you give will be highly appreciated and kept in strict confidence. We shall be pleased to reciprocate if you need our services at this end.

We are awaiting your early reply.

Yours faithfully,

(Signature)

4. 带附表的资信调查函

Dear Sirs,

We have received a sudden bid from American Trading Co., Ltd., 600 Mission Street, San Francisco, with which you are now doing business and the firm gives us your name as a reference.

We would appreciate it if you will inform us of your own experiences with the firm by filling in the blanks of the attached sheet and returning it to us in the enclosed envelope.

Any information you may give us will be treated as strictly confidential and expenses concerned from this inquiry will be gladly paid by us upon receipt of your bill.

Very truly yours,

(Signature)

Attached Sheet:

(1) How long have you been in business relations with the firm?

(2) What credit limit have you placed on their account?

(3) How promptly are terms met?

(4) What amount is currently outstanding?

5. 资信调查有利回函，给予建议

Dear Sirs,

In reply to your letter of August 18, we want to inform that we have now received from Barclay Bank of London the information you require.

The London Trading Co., Ltd. was founded in 1940 with a capital of 1,000,000 pounds. Their chief line is in the import and export of textiles. Their business' suppliers are satisfied with them. We consider them good for business engagement up to an amount of 300,000 pounds. For larger transactions we suggest payment by sight L/C.

The above information is strictly confidential and is given without any responsibility on this bank.

Truly yours,

(Signature)

6. 资信调查有利回函，告知敬请放心

Gentlemen,

The firm mentioned in your letter of September 20 is one of the most responsible dealers of textile goods.

The company was established in 1948, and has supplied our firm with qualified goods for over 20 years.

They have always provided complete satisfaction with in-time delivery, moderate prices and superior quality.

We believe that they may be rated as an A-level company with which you can deal freely. Of course, this is our personal opinion and we assume no responsibility in your proposed business negotiations.

We hope the above is satisfactory and will help you in making a decision.

Very truly yours,
(Signature)
Business Manager

7. 资信调查不利回函，告知管理不善

Dear Sirs,

We have completed our enquiries concerning the company mentioned in your letter of May 18 and have to inform you to consider carefully the business with them.

In the past three years, the company has experienced a serious difficulty in finance and delayed in executing their normal payment. It seems to us that the company's difficulties were due to bad management and in particular to overtrading.

We would advise you to pay most careful attention to any business relations with them. However, this is our personal opinion and we wish you to make further enquiries on your part.

Yours sincerely,
(Signature)

8. 资信调查不利回函，告知经济信用不佳

Dear Sirs,

We are sorry to say that our experiences with the company which you inquired about in your letter of June 17 have been unsatisfactory.

It is true we have been in business relations with the firm of the last two years and on several occasions we have had lots of trouble in effecting settlements.

The company still owes $1,400 for purchase made over seven months ago. The account is now in the hand of our attorneys for collection.

May we ask that this information should be treated as strictly confidential without responsibility on our part?

Very truly yours,

(Signature)

9. 表明无法提供确切意见而致歉

Dear Sirs,

We regret our inability to let you know any positive information concerning the firm in question in your letter of June 6.

It is true that we had business with them during the past few years, but the amount of business was not so large that we can not supply any responsible opinion on the business capability and credit standing.

We suggest you make further status enquiries from other enquiry agencies.

Yours truly,

(Signature)

10. 请求老客户作为资信证人

Dear Mr. Green,

Thank you for your letter on November 2. We are delighted to hear that you are so pleased with the refurbishment of your hotel.

As you know, in our line of work, we depend on good reports about our projects to win further business. Our clients always shop around and look for references before committing themselves.

We would like to use your hotel as a reference when we discuss similar refurbishments in the hotel industry. Would you agree to our suggestion that future clients could call you?

It would also be most helpful if we could occasionally bring a client to look at your hotel. We would, of course, stay overnight at least.

I will call you next week to hear your reaction. Thanks again for you kind words.

Yours sincerely,

(Signature)

Manager

11. 要求对方提供资信资料

Dear Sirs,

We are very glad to receive your fax inquiry. Since it is the first time we contact, we would be highly appreciated if you could provide us your bank name and address.

We realize the types of IC you need, but we do not know the specification you require for that IC such as the voltage, current. Could you please tell us the purpose of this IC?

The fax you sent us is not very clear for the wording part. Therefore, please fax it again (no need for graph).We wish we could provide the best services for you.

Sincerely yours,

(Signature)

12. 同意试销前的资信要求

Dear Sirs,

Thank you for your letter on 10th March. We are gratified to receive your request for men's and women's raincoats on approval.

As we have not previously done business together, perhaps you will kindly agree to supply either the usual trade references, or the name of a bank to which we may refer. As soon as these enquiries are satisfactorily settled, we shall be happy to send you the items you mention in your letter.

We sincerely hope this will be the beginning of a long and pleasant business association. We shall do our best to make it so.

Yours,

(Signature)

Topic discussion:

1. What factors should be taken into consideration when writing a letter for credit information?

2. If you can not give a positive information about the the firm in question, what will you do?

其他常用词汇和短语

audio inquiry 声频询问, 声音回答, 声音询问

banking credit 银行信用

bear inquiry 经得起追问

commercial credit 商业信用

credit inquiry 商业信用调查

credit inquiry division 信用咨询组

design of statistical inquiry 统计调查设计

hold an inquiry into 对……进行调查

inquiry office 问询处

on inquiry 经调查, 经询问

Unit

5

Order and Confirm

订单与确认

Learning Resources

Warming-up

An order is a request to supply a specified quantity of goods. Very often, it is only after the exchange of a number of letters, faxes or e-mails that the two parties come entirely to terms and the buyer finally places or fills a formal order by letter or fax. Sometimes a buyer may take the initiative by placing a firm order with the seller, which is a firm bid to buy something and contains all the necessary terms and conditions. When a seller receives the relative order and confirms and accepts its terms and conditions, he may begin to execute the order to the buyer's satisfaction.

Dialogues

 **Dialogue 1** **Placing a Trial Order**

Ms. Terry (T) wants to order some products from Mr. Higgon (H). Now, they are talking over the issue of price.

H: What particular items are you interested in?

T: I'm interested in Article A66 for the moment. I'd like to order four hundred thousand yards of Article A66 for prompt shipment.

H: I'm afraid it won't be available till September. If you are in urgent need of the goods, I'd like to recommend Article 88. It is very similar and even superior to A66.

T: Can I see any sample cutting here? Mmm… the quality is not bad. Would you give me your idea of price?

H: The price is $2 per yard CIF European Main Ports.

T: Is there any commission included?

H: No, as a rule, we don't allow any commission. But if the order is large enough, we will consider it.

T: As this is a trial order, I hope you will give me a special consideration.

H: Well, in order to encourage the business, we'll allow you 2% commission, that's the best

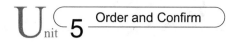

we can do.

T: Thank you. We'll place an order for 400,000 yards of A88. I think this is the maximum quantity we can place now. I hope it can reach us within two months.

H: We ensure timely delivery of the goods. Thank you, our talk has been a successful one.

▶ Dialogue 2 Ordering Motorcycles

Miss Anne (A) prepares to order a batch of motorcycles, and she is asking Ms. Claffy (C), the supplier of motorcycles, to explain the specification of the motorcycles.

A: It looks nice. Let me have the particular.

C: Model BM-22, 4 stroke, 120 cc.

A: Say! That's three times more than the other one. Does it develop three times the power?

C: Just about three times. The tested rating is 12 horse-powers and the speed is 110 kph.

A: Now we come to quantity. This will be the major selling line, I'm sure, so we will take 2,000 motorcycles.

C: Are you ready to take any more of the Scooter type?

A: I think we'll give them a rest for a while. Might be able to take some later this year. This 2,000 is about our limit for the present.

C: I see. Well, where is the destination port?

A: I think you'd better ship half to Liverpool and half to London.

C: Right. I'll get our dispatch department started on the packing.

A: Yes, please do. And I'll prepare an official order from these notes and send it to you tomorrow. How's that?

C: That'll be fine, thank you.

▶ Dialogue 3 A Trial Order for Electronic Toys

American businessman Colin Hill (H) is very interested in Chinese electronic animal toys. So, after rounds of negotiations, he decides to place a trial order with Ms. Li (L), the exporter's representative.

H: Hello, Ms. Li. We decide to place a trial order with you. We want to order C-46 and C-48 series of electronic animal toys, each series for 5,000 pieces.

L: Mr. Hill, the former series are in stock while stocks of the latter have been sold out. It will be at least two weeks before they are available again. You know, we have many back orders.

H: Can you recommend other similar ones?

L: Another make C-24 that you saw yesterday is in stock. It is similar in design and quality to C-48. And the price is also the same. It is reported that C-24 is more popular with young girls.

H: Thank you. Well, I'll take your advice and order C-46 and C-24 for 5,000 each. Just a moment, I'll fill in my order form. Here is our order No. 0506.

L: Thank you for your initial order and I expect to have your further orders.

H: We will, perhaps next month, if your price is competitive.

L: Then as one of our regular customers, you will enjoy the special discount of 10%.

Dialogue 4 Placing a Trial Order for Computers

Indian businessman, Mr. Singer (S), places a trial order for 300 computers after further discussions on the price issue and other terms and conditions with Ms. Gongxin (G), sales manager of Hitch Co., Ltd.

S: I'm glad that we have finally reached an agreement on the price issue and on other terms and conditions.

G: Me too. Do you have any intention to place a trial order?

S: Well, yes, and I have come to place a trial order with you.

G: Thank you very much, Mr. Singer.

S: I fell in love with the design and configuration of your computers when I saw your samples.

G: How many do you have in mind to order?

S: We want to order 300 sets for a trial sale.

G: Do you think we need to review the detailed terms and conditions of our deal?

S: No, as they are agreed upon and written in the Order Sheet. We're ordering 300 DP4000 PCs at US$560 each FOB Dalian. Payment is to be made by irrevocable, confirmed L/C. How soon will shipment be effected?

G: Within one month after receipt of your L/C. Will you take partial deliveries?

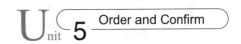
S: No problem. Here is our order form for a trial order. Everything is written here.

G: Good. Everything seems correct. And please wait for a moment. I'll get our order acceptance ready.

Words and Expressions

in stock 有库存	老主顾
back order 积压的订单，到期尚未	special discount 特别折扣
执行的订单	place a trial order with 向……试购
recommend *v.* 推荐	fall in love with 开始喜欢某物
design *n.* 款式	configuration *n.* 配置
order form 订购单	have in mind 意欲，打算
initial order 首次订购，初订单	partial delivery 分批交货，分批装运
regular customer 老顾客，常客，	order acceptance 订单确认书

Notes

1. 订购

订购是交易中的一个重要环节，尽管买卖双方在正式订购之前就价格及其他交易条件已经进行过反复磋商并达成了一致意见，但各种潜在的问题往往在订购之后才能反映出来。而错误的订购将会导致企业的亏损甚至破产。因此，买方在发订单时一定要慎之又慎，作为首次交易，最好采用试购的方式订购。

订购有一些具体的形式，包括订购函、制式订单（订购合同）、传真单和网上购物单等。从当今及今后贸易发展的趋势来看，传真单和网上购物单将是订单使用的两种主要形式。无论何种订单，其基本内容是相同的，但企业最好还是采用其独特的统一的格式，这样可使订购工作方便、清晰，易于操作。

2. I'd like to order four hundred thousand yards of Article A66 for prompt shipment.
   我想订购 40 万码，而且需即期付运。

3. Well, in order to encourage the business, we'll allow you 2% commission, that's the best we can do. 好吧，为了鼓励贸易，我们给你 2% 的佣金，不能再多了。

4. kph 千米每小时（"kilometer per hour" 的缩写形式）

5. This 2,000 is about our limit for the present.

这 2 000 辆是我们现在所能订购的最大数量。

6. You know, we have many back orders.

   您知道，我们积压了很多订单。

7. ...I expect to have your further orders.

   ……希望您下次再订。

8. Then as one of our regular customers, you will enjoy the special discount of 10%.

   那么，作为我们的固定客户之一，您会享受 10% 的特别折扣。

9. I'll get our order acceptance ready.

   我给你准备一份订单确认书。

Useful Sentences

1. We are pleased to give you an order for 3,000 computers in current stock at the prices you quoted.

   根据你方报价，我们向你方下了 3 000 台现有库存计算机的订单。

2. We wish to order from you your products as per our purchase.

   我方希望能按照订货单订购贵方产品。

3. We are pleased to place with you an order for 2,000 washing machines to be supplied from current stock.

   我们向贵方下了 2 000 台洗衣机的订单，希望现货供应。

4. We wish to order from you according to this purchase order.

   根据这个采购单我们向贵方下订单。

5. Thank you for your quotation dated May 20th. And this is our official order for 10 palace lanterns.

   感谢您 5 月 20 日的报价，这是我们 10 只宫灯的正式订单。

6. We are glad to inform you that your samples are satisfactory, we'd like to order 4 of the items.

   很高兴通知您，我们对贵方的样品非常满意，我们想向贵方订购样品中的 4 款产品。

7. If the quality is up to our expectations, we shall send further orders in the near future.

   若质量达到我们的期望，我们将在近期向贵方下新订单。

8. We find both the price and quality of your products satisfactory to our client and we are pleased to give you an order for the items on this sheet.

   我们发现贵方产品在价格和质量上均能使我们的客户满意，我们向贵方下该表格中此类别产品的订单。

9. We should be glad if you would accept our order for coffee whose number is No. 3003.

如果贵方能够接受编号为 3003 的咖啡订单，我们将很高兴。

10. We'd like to place an order with you for 1,000 cases each of No. 77 and 100 at $5 and $6 FOB Shanghai.

我们将向贵方订购编号为 77 和 100 的产品各 1 000 箱，单价分别为 5 美金和 6 美金，上海离岸价。

11. What is the minimum quantity of an order for your goods?

贵方产品的最小订货量是多少？

12. I am trusted to place an order for 100 sewing machines at $250 each.

我们确认订购 100 台缝纫机，价格为每台 250 美金。

13. This is our official trial order for 500 computers.

这是我们 500 台计算机的正式试订单。

14. If you can fill our order of 5,000 ties very soon we'd like to place the order with you now.

若你们能迅速供应 5 000 条领带的话，我们现在就下订单给你。

15. We hope that you can accept the order in the buyer's design and measurement.

我们希望贵方能够接受买方设计和尺寸的订单。

16. We will send you the order very soon, please hurry to execute it.

我们将很快下订单给你方，请赶紧执行订单。

17. The order is so urgently required that we must ask you to make the earliest possible shipment.

该订单急需，我们要求你方必须尽早装船。

18. We are glad to receive your order and confirm the acceptance of it.

我们很高兴接到你方的订单并且确认可以接受。

19. This is our sales confirmation concerning your order No. 26 of April 10th.

这是关于你方 4 月 10 日订购编号 26 产品的销售确认书。

20. We acknowledged your order of May 5th for 100 units of motorcycle P180.

我们接受你方 5 月 5 日所下的 100 台型号为 P180 的摩托车订单。

21. We regret that owing to the shortage of stocks we are unable to fill your order.

很遗憾因为库存不足我们不能完成你方的订单。

22. We feel great regret that we can no longer supply the goods you order as the production has been discontinued since last August.

非常遗憾我们不再供应订单上的货物，因为生产已于八月停止。

23. At present, we can not undertake to entertain your order owing to the uncertain availability of raw materials.

目前由于原材料供应的不确定性，我们无法承诺完成你方的订单。

24. We regret that we are unable to meet your requirements for the time being as orders have been fully booked.

因为订单已满，我们很遗憾目前无法满足你方的要求。

25. We are too heavily committed to be able to entertain fresh orders.

我们手中有大量订货，无法接受新的订单。

I Complete the following dialogues.

1. **A:** Should you favor me with your orders?

   B: _____.

   （请尽快给我们送 20 匹布来。）

2. **A:** Thank you for your bottom price.

   B: _____.

   （我希望能得到你更多的订单。）

3. **A:** _____?

   （你们怎样包装我们订的碗？）

   B: We would use wooden cases for packing.

4. **A:** _____?

   （你想订多少？）

   B: 400 pairs.

5. **A:** How should we settle the payment?

   B: _____.

   （金额大的订货，我们要求开信用证。）

II Situational practice.

Make dialogues according to the following situations.

1. Andy worked in a large shopping center. He had placed an order for 400 pairs of women's shoes. However, to his surprise, he received 300 pairs of children's shoes 10 days later. The shoes were completely not in accordance with those ordered. He contacted the manufacturer immediately and made a complaint. Finally, the problem was satisfactorily solved.

2. Harry, a sales manager, has just received an order for 1,500 mobile phones from one of his regular customers. This customer owes him $6,000 for his last purchase. Now, the customer asks for one month's credit for the purchase this time. Harry has been placed in a dilemma. Finally, he decides to offer him the phones on credit.

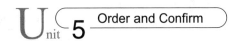
对话汉译

▶ **对话 1** 产品试订

特丽女士（T）想从希根先生（H）处订购一些货物。现在，他们正就价格问题进行磋商。

H：你对什么产品感兴趣呢？

T：我对 A66 号产品很感兴趣，目前想订购 40 万码，而且需即期付运。

H：恐怕 9 月份之前无货，如果你急需的话，我为你推荐类似的 A88 号产品，其质量优于 A66。

T：我能看样品吗？嗯，质量不错，价格如何？

H：每码 2 美元，欧洲主要港口到岸价。

T：包括佣金吗？

H：不包括，一般我们是不给佣金的。但如果订货量大，我们也可以考虑。

T：由于这是试订货，你们能否给予特别考虑？

H：好吧，为了鼓励业务往来，我们给你 2% 的佣金，不能再多了。

T：谢谢，我们订 40 万码 A88 号产品。我想这是我们现在所能订购的最大数量。我希望货物能在两个月内到达。

H：我保证及时送货。谢谢，我们的商谈非常成功。

▶ **对话 2** 订购摩托车

安妮小姐（A）准备订购一批摩托车。她正在向供应商克拉菲女士（C）询问摩托车的规格。

A：这部车子看来不错，请告诉我它的规格细目。

C：BM-22 型，四冲程，气缸容量 120 cc。

A：哦！那是另一种摩托车的三倍。它的马力也是另一种的 3 倍吗？

C：正好是 3 倍，测试等级是 12 马力，时速为 110 公里。

A：现在我们来谈谈数量问题，我相信这种摩托车将成为主力销售类型，因此我们想订购 2 000 台这种摩托车。

C：你准备多订购一些小型摩托车吗？

A：暂时先不考虑，可能今年下半年会订购。这 2 000 台是我们公司目前的最高订购限度。

C：我明白了。那么，目的港是哪里？

A：我想你们最好一半货至利物浦，另一半至伦敦。

C：好的。我会指示配送部门开始包装。

A：好的，麻烦你了。我将从这些摘要中整理出一份正式订单，明天寄给你，如何？

C：那很好，谢谢你！

▶ 对话 3 试订电子玩具

美国商人科林•希尔（H）对中国的电子动物玩具很感兴趣，经几轮磋商之后，决定向出口商代表李女士（L）发试订单。

H：您好，李女士。我们决定向您发试订单。我们想订购 C-46 和 C-48 系列电子动物玩具，各 5 000 个。

L：希尔先生，您所订的前一种型号有库存，但后一种已经卖完。至少要两周以后才有货。您知道，我们积压了很多订单。

H：您能推荐其他类似的玩具吗？

L：昨天您看的另一种款式 C-24 有现货，与 C-48 型在款式和质量上相似。据报告，C-24 型在小女孩中更为流行。

H：谢谢。好吧，我接受您的建议，订购 C-46 型和 C-24 型，各 5 000 个。等一下，我要填写订单。这是我们的第 0506 号订单。

L：谢谢您向我们首次订购，期待您有更多的订单。

H：我们会的，或许下个月，如果你们的价格具有竞争力的话。

L：那时，作为我们的老主顾之一，您会享受 10%的特别折扣。

▶ 对话 4 试订计算机

印度客商泰特斯•辛格先生（S）与 Hitch 有限公司的销售部经理龚昕女士（G）对价格等问题进行深入的磋商之后，决定试购 300 台计算机。

S：非常高兴我们就价格等条件达成了一致意见。

G：我也是。您想试订一些产品吗？

S：哦，是的，我此次前来，正是向贵公司试购的。

G：多谢，辛格先生。

S：看样品的时候，我就喜欢你们计算机的款式和配置。

G：你们打算订购多少呢？

S：我们想订购 300 台试销。

G：我们要不要回顾一下具体的交易条件？

S：不用了，我们都达成一致并写在订单里了。我们将订购 300 台 DP4000 型计算机，每台大连离岸价 560 美元，以不可撤销的保兑信用证支付。此货最快能在何时装运？

G：收到信用证后一个月之内，你们是否可以接受分批装运？

S：没问题。这是我们的试购单，都写在上面了。

G：很好，一切就绪。请等一下，我给你准备一份订单确认书。

Extended Reading

Order and Confirm

After rounds of negotiation, both the seller and the buyer finally agree on the revised terms and conditions. The buyer then places an order with the seller. An order is a request to supply goods or services on terms and conditions agreed upon. Orders can be given orally or in written form, for instance, telephone conversations, talks at a meeting, letters, printed forms or memorandums.

When an order is placed, such basic information as full details of name of commodity, model number, specifications, unit and total prices, quantities etc. should be given. Also the mode of packing, method of shipment, shipping mark, destination and insurance should be clearly stated. Then the one who is placing the order should once again confirm the terms of payment as agreed upon. When the buyer sends the order, he also sends a confirmation of purchase in duplicate to be countersigned, with one copy to be returned for file.

Having received an order from the buyer, the seller should immediately send an acknowledgement or acceptance which includes the seller's thanks for the order, assurance of prompt and careful attention, promise to adhere to the terms and conditions agreed upon, favorable comment on the goods ordered, and hopes for further orders. The seller should also send a confirmation of sales in duplicate to be countersigned.

Topic discussion:

1. What basic information should be included in an order?

2. What should we do to convince our clients when answering an order?

其他常用词汇和短语

amended order　修改后的订单

business booth　洽谈室

commercial invoice　卖方发票，商业发票

conclude　*v.* 结束，议定

cooperation　*n.* 合作

excuse　*n.* 借口，理由

finalize a transaction　达成交易

for our file　供我方存档

force majeure　不可抗力

frequent　*a.* 时常发生的

interval　*n.* （时间的）间隔

make signature　签字

non-negotiable　不能议付的，非流通的

origin　*n.* 原产地

original　*n.* 原件

prompt　*a.* 立刻的，迅速的

sailing　*n.* 航行，开船

sales confirmation　销售确认书

sales contract　销售合同

shipping mark　唛头

telex　*v.* 发用户电报
　　　n. 用户直通电报

terms and conditions　交易条件

transship　*v.* 转船运输

trial order　试订单

Unit

6

Payment

支 付

Learning Resources

Warming-up

Just as in domestic trade, any transaction in international trade, large or small, has to be settled through payment by the buyer. However, payment in international trade is often beset with more difficulties owing to the fact that either party to a business transaction has relatively limited knowledge of the financial strength and commercial reputation of his counterpart. To guarantee the punctual delivery on the part of the seller and payment by the buyer, different modes of payments have been created, which can be divided into three categories, illustrated as follows: remittance; collection; letter of credit (L/C).

Remittance and collection belong to commercial credit, but letter of credit belongs to the banker's credit.

As far as the seller's benefit is concerned, L/C is better than collection, and collection is better than remittance. When collection is adopted, D/P at sight is better than D/P after sight, whereas D/P is better than D/A.

Dialogues

▶ Dialogue 1 **Negotiating the Terms of Payment (I)**

Porter (P) and Gloria (G) are negotiating the terms of payment.

P: Gloria, I am sorry to say that the only term of payment we can accept is 100% irrevocable documentary letter of credit.

G: Opening an L/C is not a problem. But as you know, you always request us to open L/C at sight, but your date of delivery is always 35 days after your receipt of the L/C. I think this is not fair.

P: Gloria, L/C at sight is what we request for all our customers. As for the date of delivery, I think we can discuss it.

G: Porter, you have to understand that in America time is very important to us. We always hope you can deliver the goods as soon as you receive our L/C. I know it's impossible for you to deliver the goods immediately after your receipt of our L/C, but please don't let us wait for 35 days.

P: Actually, it is not because we want you to wait, it is because we need time to arrange transportation. For example, inland transportation of the goods to the port, sometimes takes three to four weeks and before we receive the L/C we normally don't arrange transportation. I hope you can understand us.

G: I understand, but I know you can do something.

P: The only thing I can do is to deliver the goods 25 days after we receive your L/C.

G: OK. Make it 25 days. Then I will put it in L/C that goods should be delivered 25 days upon your receipt of L/C.

P: OK. But when do you think your L/C will arrive?

G: I think it will come soon. I'll send a fax to my company right now. I'm sure they will push our bank.

P: If you need an early delivery of goods, you have to tell your bank to open the L/C as soon as possible.

G: I understand this.

P: Will your bank open the L/C by mail or by telex?

G: Normally by mail, but if you want to save time, it can also be done by telex, but we have to pay a bit more.

P: I understand it now.

G: I'll tell my company that the L/C should arrive within 15 days and let them decide what to do, OK?

P: That's very good.

 **Dialogue 2** **Placing an Order on the Phone**

Superworth Trading Co. in a foreign country has a long standing contractual cooperation with Huanghai Furniture; therefore, they usually settle their accounts by remittance. (Miss Helen Faulkner (F), purchaser from Superworth Trading Co.; Miss Zheng Yuan (Z), secretary of the Imp. & Exp. Department of Huanghai Furniture; Mr. Han Weitai (H), manager of the Imp. & Exp. Department of Huanghai Furniture)

Z: Huanghai Furniture, Zheng Yuan speaking.

F: Hi, Miss Zheng. It's me, Helen from Superworth Trading Co.

Z: Oh, hi, Helen, it's nice to hear you.

F: Can I speak to your manager, Mr. Han?

Z: Just a moment, please.

H: Hello, Han is speaking.

F: We've just received your sample of the new assembly coffee table and are quite satisfied with it.

H: Oh, it's very kind of you to say so. Can we expect an order from you?

F: Yes, that's why I'm making the call. I'm placing an order for the new assembly coffee tables of both the padauk and mahogany finishes for 500 sets separately, with a total of 1,000 sets. Please take care that the goods are carefully packed.

H: No problem. We insured them against damage.

F: Can you make the delivery before the end of this month?

H: We have the tables in stock. There will be no trouble at all for us to deliver them within this month.

F: Good. Can we settle the account by T/T, as usual?

H: Yes, of course.

▶ Dialogue 3   Negotiating the Terms of Payment (II)

Ms. Snow (S) is negotiating over the terms of payment with Mr. Fu Ming (F), sales manager of Yida Trading Company.

S: Mr. Fu, as this is not the first transaction between us and the amount is not very big, we'd like to ask you to give us favorable terms. Payment by L/C, you know, will involve additional expenses for us, and as a result, will leave us no margin of profit.

F: Ms. Snow, you know quite well that our goods enjoy an excellent reputation in the international market. The goods you are interested in are sold quite well. I'm sure the quick turnover will not only offset your L/C expenses but also give you a satisfactory profit.

S: But as far as I know, Mr. Fu, you sometimes grant your regular customers favorable terms, such as remittance.

F: Occasionally we do. But it is only under very special circumstances that we agree to these payment terms.

S: That's good, Mr. Fu. You see, such a small order as ours doesn't belong to a normal case, doesn't it? We hope you will agree to our making payment by mail transfer.

F: Mmm… Well, Ms. Snow, in view of our long-standing cooperation, we agree to T/T payment. I think that is the best we can do.

S: OK, thank you for your consideration.

F: We would suggest that for this particular order you remit a 10% down payment to us by T/T, on receipt of which we shall ship the goods on the first steamer available, with the balance to be paid by T/T not later than November 10th.

S: I think that's OK. Thank you for granting us this facility.

▶ Dialogue 4 Payment in Installment

Mr. Li (L) is talking about the terms of payment with Ms. Anne (A).

L: So far, this order valued at $500,000, we pay in installments. That is, payment will be spread over five shipments during the five years.

A: That's right. But you should issue a time draft for $200,000 covering the value of the first partial shipment.

L: I see. By the way, when will the draft fall due?

A: On May 31, 2012. Please see that the draft for the first partial shipment will reach us for our acceptance at the time of the contract being signed.

L: Surely we will.

A: As to the goods, we'll send them to your country in five different lots within five years.

L: Delivered by June 30th each year, right?

A: Yes. And I have to mention that, for our acceptance, you should issue a draft for the next partial shipment after we deliver the last goods, so that we may arrange the shipment.

L: OK.

Words and Expressions

irrevocable *a.* 不能取消的，不能撤回的	offset *v.* 弥补，抵消
padauk *n.* 紫檀	long-standing *a.* 长期的
mahogany *n.* 红木	down payment 预付定金，首付款
finish *n.* （家具等表面的）罩面	receipt *n.* 收到，收讫
margin of profit 边际利润，利润限度	steamer *n.* 轮船
installment *n.* 分期付款	balance *n.* 余款，余额
turnover *n.* 周转量，周转额	facility *n.* 便利

Notes

1. 汇付

在国际贸易中，汇付属于商业信用，受合同的约束，但不受银行信用的保护。所谓"信用"，在国际贸易中是指由谁承担付款和递交单证。在汇付方式中，买方负责付款，卖方负责递交单证。

采用汇付方式时，卖方一般希望采用电汇。几年前电汇一般采用电报、电传方式，现在一般采用 SWIFT 方式。电汇的特点是快捷、安全，有利于卖方及时收回货款，加速资金周转，避免汇率变动风险。而采用汇付方式时，买方则希望采用信汇，因为采用信汇时，买方不必支付额外的电报费用和其他银行费用。

2. Then I will put it in L/C that goods should be delivered 25 days upon your receipt of L/C.

那么我将在信用证中写上你方在收到信用证后 25 天内发货。

3. I'm sure they will push our bank.

我保证他们会敦促银行尽快办理的。

4. Please take care that the goods are carefully packed.

请注意对商品认真地进行包装。

5. We insured them against damage.

我们已经投了损坏险。

6. ...We'd like to ask you to give us favorable terms.

……我们想请求您给我们提供优惠条件。

7. Payment by L/C, you know, will involve additional expenses for us, and as a result, will leave us no margin of profit.

您知道，信用证支付将会给我们增加额外费用，结果是，我方将无利可言。

8. I'm sure the quick turnover will not only offset your L/C expenses but also give you a satisfactory profit.

我相信，快速的周转不仅能补偿你方信用证的费用，而且还会使您赚到满意的利润。

9. ...for this particular order you remit a 10% down payment to us by T/T ...

……对这次特别的订购，建议你方电汇 10%的首期付款……

10. ...we pay in installments.

……我们采用分期付款的方式。

Useful Sentences

1. Payment is to be effected (made) before the end of this month.

这个月底之前应该付款。

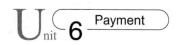
2. It's convenient to make payment in pound sterling.
   用英镑付款较方便。

3. Now, as regards payment, we've agreed to use US dollar, am I right?
   至于付款，我们已同意用美元，对吗？

4. We may have some difficulties making payment in Japanese yen.
   用日元付款可能会有困难。

5. I've never made payment in RMB before.
   我从未用人民币付过款。

6. We can't accept payment on deferred terms.
   我们不能接受延期付款。

7. What's your reason for the refusal of payment?
   你们拒付的理由是什么？

8. Collection is not paid.
   托收款未付。

9. We don't think you'll refuse to pay.
   我们相信你们不会拒付。

10. Only one refusal of payment is acceptable to the bank.
    银行只接受一次拒付。

11. You ought to pay us the bank interest once payment is wrongly refused.
    如果拒付错了，你们应该偿付我方的银行利息。

12. We'll not pay until shipping documents for the goods have reached us.
    见不到货物装船单据，我们不付款。

13. We're worried that a decline in prices might lead to refusal of payment.
    我们担心市场价格下跌会引起拒付。

14. Of course, payment might be refused if anything goes wrong with the documents.
    如果单据有问题，当然可以提出拒付。

15. The equipment will be paid in installments with the commodities produced by our factory.
    设备以我们工厂生产的产品分期偿还。

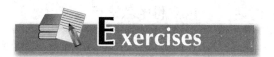

Exercises

I Complete the following dialogues.

1. **A:** Let's decide on the terms of payment.

B: _____.

（好的，那正是我想要谈到的。）

2. **A:** _____.

（好吧，从长计议，这一次我们接受承兑交单，但下不为例。）

B: Thank you very much for your application.

3. **A:** Could you think about your terms of payment once again?

B: _____.

（恐怕不行，我们采取这种方式是为了与国际惯例保持一致。）

4. **A:** As the peak season is coming, we would like you to deliver by October.

B: _____.

（我们保证能够做到。）

5. **A:** _____.

（若贵方未能按时付款，我方将终止合同。）

B: You can rest assured that.

II Situational practice.

Make dialogues according to the following situations.

1. Tony and Blair are discussing the terms of payment of a transaction. Tony requires the payment of D/P or D/A, but Blair insists on payment by open, confirmed, irrevocable L/C. At last Tony breaks the ice and accepts the terms of Blair. Meanwhile, Blair promises to deliver the goods as soon as possible.

2. Before Tom and Berry are going to visit Pudong New District, Tom suggests paying Berry by means of D/P or D/A, but Berry sticks to the payment by L/C. They can't reach an agreement and promise to talk about it the next day.

对话汉译

▶ 对话 1 就支付条款进行磋商（一）

波特（P）正在与格洛丽亚（G）就支付条款进行谈判。

P: 格洛丽亚，抱歉地说，我们能接受的付款条件只有100% 不可能撤销跟单信用证。

G: 开立信用证不成问题。但是你知道，你方一直要求我们开立即期信用证，可是交货

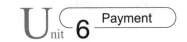

期总是在你方收到信用证之后的 35 天。我想这不公平。

P: 格洛丽亚，即期信用证是我方对所有顾客的要求。至于交货日期，我想我们可以讨论。

G: 波特，你应当理解，在美国，时间对我们来说非常重要。我们总希望你们一收到我方信用证就立即交货。我知道这对于你们来说是不可能的，但是拜托你们不要让我们等 35 天。

P: 事实上，不是我们想让你们等，而是我们需要时间来安排运输。比如从内陆运输货物到港口有时需要 3 到 4 周，但在我方收到信用证之前，我们通常不安排运输。我希望你能理解。

G: 我理解，不过我知道你们能想些办法。

P: 我方唯一能做的就是在我方收到你方信用证后 25 天发货。

G: 好的，那就 25 天。那么我将在信用证中写上你方在收到信用证后 25 天内发货。

P: 好的。不过，你方的信用证何时能到？

G: 我想很快就能到。我立刻往公司发一份传真。我保证他们会督促银行尽快办理的。

P: 如果你们要早点装运，那么你就必须告诉你方银行尽快开立信用证。

G: 我明白。

P: 你方银行是用信函还是用电报开立信用证？

G: 通常采用信函方式，但如果你们想节约时间，也可采取电报方式。不过我方将多付一些费用。

P: 现在我明白了。

G: 我将告诉公司信用证应在 15 天内到达，然后让他们决定怎样去做，好吗？

P: 很好。

▶ 对话 2　通过电话下订单

国外的 Superworth 贸易公司与黄海家具公司有着长期的合作合同，所以他们一般通过汇付方式结账。[海伦·福克纳小姐（F），Superworth 贸易公司的采购员；郑媛小姐（Z），黄海家具公司进出口部秘书；韩伟太先生（H），黄海家具公司进出口部经理]

Z: 这里是黄海家具公司，我是郑媛。

F: 您好，郑小姐，是我，Superworth 贸易公司的海伦。

Z: 哦，您好，海伦，很高兴接到您的电话。

F: 请帮我找一下你们的经理韩先生，好吗？

Z: 请稍等。

H: 您好，我是韩伟太。

F: 我们刚收到你们的新组合咖啡桌样品，觉得很满意。

H: 听您这么说真是太好了。您能订货吗？

F: 是的，我正是为这件事打电话的。我要订紫檀面和红木面的新组合咖啡桌，各 500 套，总计 1 000 套。请注意对商品认真地进行包装。

H: 没问题。我们已经投了损坏险。

F: 你们这个月末能交货吗？

H: 我们有库存，月内交货没问题。

F: 太好了，我们这次能否像以往一样通过电汇结账？

H: 当然可以。

▶ 对话 3　就支付条款进行磋商（二）

斯诺女士（S）与亿达贸易公司销售部经理付明先生（F）就支付条款一事进行磋商。

S: 付先生，由于这不是我们之间的第一笔交易，况且这次的订购数量也不太大，我们想请求您给我们提供优惠条件。您知道，信用证支付将会给我们增加额外费用，结果是，我方将无利可言。

F: 斯诺女士，您知道我们的商品在国际市场上备受青睐。您看中的商品销路很好。我相信，快速的周转不仅能补偿你方信用证的费用，而且还会使您赚到满意的利润。

S: 但据我所知，付先生，贵方有时会给予老客户优惠的条件，比方说汇付。

F: 是的，我们偶尔这样做。只是在非常特殊的情况下我们才同意采用这些支付方式。

S: 这很好，付先生。您瞧，像我这样小的订单不属于正常情况，对吧？希望贵方同意我方以信汇方式付款。

F: 嗯……，那好吧，斯诺女士，鉴于我们长期的合作，我方同意采用电汇的付款方式。我想我们不能再作让步了。

S: 好吧，谢谢您的关照。

F: 对这次特别的订购，建议你方电汇 10% 的首期付款，接到付款后我们将把货物装在第一艘轮船上。余额用电汇方式支付，不得晚于 11 月 10 日。

S: 没问题。感谢您的通融。

▶ 对话 4　分期付款

李先生（L）正在就付款方式与安妮女士（A）进行磋商。

L: 这样，我们这批价值 50 万美元的货物将采用分期付款的方式，即在 5 年内分 5 次支付。

A: 是的。不过别忘了先开具一张价值 20 万美元的远期汇票用于支付第一批货物。

L: 知道了。顺便问一下，期票何时到期？

A: 2012 年 5 月 31 日。支付第一批货物的远期汇票请务必在签合同之时给我方承兑。

L: 当然。

A: 关于货物，我方将在 5 年内分 5 次向贵国发运。

L: 在每年 6 月 30 日交货，对吗？

A: 是的。请注意，在每批货交付你方后，你方应尽快开一张期票给我方承兑，以便我们安排下一批货装运。

L: 好的。

Extended Reading

Payment Terms

In international business, any transaction, large or small, has to be settled through payment. Payment is the final goal of all business activities. Without payment business would be meaningless. In order to guarantee payment by the buyer and punctual delivery by the seller, proper methods of payment should be chosen. In international business, remittance, collection and letter of credit are three main modes of payment. When remittance is adopted, the buyer should remit the money to the seller on his own initiative, and the seller should send the goods to the buyer according to the terms and time stipulated in the contract. Remittance belongs to the commercial credit. Remittance includes mail transfer (M/T), telegraphic transfer (T/T), and demand draft (D/D). Under M/T the buyer gives the money of the goods to his local bank. The local bank then issues a trust deed for payment and sends it to a correspondent bank at the seller's end by means of mail. The seller can get the money in his place. Under T/T, payment is transferred by means of cable through the bank to the seller. Under D/D, the buyer buys a bank draft from his local bank and sends it by mail to the seller and the seller takes the money in his place.

Topic discussion:

1. How many major payment terms are there in the international business?

2. What payment term(s) do you prefer in international business?

其他常用词汇和短语

cash against aocuments（CAD） 凭单付现

cash on delivery（COD） 交货付现

cash with order（CWO） 随订单付现

clean payment 单纯支付

decline *v.* 下降，下跌

deferred payment 延期付款

dishonor *v.* 拒付

pay *v.* 付款，支付，偿还

pay... Co. or order （pay to the order of... Co.） 付……公司或其指定人

pay... Co. not negotiable 付……公司，不准疏通

pay... Co. only 仅付……公司

pay on delivery（POD） 货到付款

pay order 支付凭证

payment agreement 支付协定

payment at maturity 到期付款

payment by banker 银行支付

payment by installment 分期付款

payment by remittance 汇拨支付

payment for（in）cash 现金支付，付现

payment in advance 预付（货款）

payment in full 全部付讫

payment in kind 实物支付

payment in part 部分付款

payment on terms 定期付款，按条件付款

payment order 付款通知

payment respite 延期付款

progressive payment 分期付款

refusal *n.* 拒绝

simple payment 单纯支付

something goes wrong 某事上出了问题，在某事上出现差错

the bank interest 银行利息

the refusal of payment 拒付

Unit

7

Business Logistics
商务物流

Learning Resources

Warming-up

Logistics as a business concept evolved in the 1950s due to the increasing complexity of supplying businesses with materials and shipping out products in an increasingly globalized supply chain, leading to a call for experts called supply chain logisticians. Business logistics can be defined as "having the right item in the right quantity at the right time at the right place for the right price in the right condition to the right customer", and is the science of process and incorporates all industry sectors. The goal of logistics work is to manage the fruition of project life cycles, supply chains and resultant efficiencies.

In business, logistics may have either internal focus (inbound logistics), or external focus (outbound logistics) covering the flow and storage of materials from point of origin to point of consumption. The main functions of a qualified logistician include inventory management, purchasing, transportation, warehousing, consultation and the organizing and planning of these activities. Logisticians combine a professional knowledge of each of these functions to coordinate resources in an organization. There are two fundamentally different forms of logistics: one optimizes a steady flow of material through a network of transport links and storage nodes; the other coordinates a sequence of resources to carry out some project.

Dialogues

 **Dialogue 1** **Suggestion for the Packing**

Ms. Green (G) made a visit to the toys factory and then discussed some problems about packing with Mr. Xu (X), Mr. Green's toy products supplier.

G: Mr. Xu, we have visited the factories and I'm very satisfied with your factories' production conditions.

X: Well, they are our main export bases of toys with the advantage of having good production experience and long historical record. All our products enjoy high prestige in the world market.

G: Your products are good, and there's no question of that. But your packing needs improvement. Do you mind if I give you a little suggestion?

X: No, I don't mind. Go head.

G: We both know that one important function of packing is to stimulate the buyer's desire to buy. He should fall in love with your product at the first sight.

X: You can say that again. But could you be more specific?

G: In fact, each toy packed in a plastic bag and then packed in a cardboard box with beautiful designs in bright colors will be wonderful in our market. The design of packing is nice, but I hope you could make some improvement in color. Children like rich and fresh colors. Here is our suggestion for the packing.

X: That's really a good idea. We will do our best to suit children's taste. I'll pass your suggestion to our manufacturers and ask them to improve on it. I hope the new packing could better meet your demand.

G: I hope so. About the outer packing then, how are you going to handle that?

X: Well, we'll reinforce all those cardboard cartons with straps outside, and mark them with the words such as "Handle with care" and other general marks for transportation.

G: I'm glad to hear that. By the way, do you accept neutral packing?

X: Yes, we can pack the goods according to your instructions. Do you have any other questions or demands regarding packing?

G: No, nothing else, Mr. Xu.

X: Now let's have a short rest before we go on to the next point, shall we?

G: Sure.

X: Please have a cup of coffee.

G: Thanks.

 **Dialogue 2** **Negotiating the Shipment**

Mr. Dandy (D) is planning to ship the whole lot at one time, but Ms. Wang (W) suggests partial shipment be allowed.

W: Mr. Dandy, I'm afraid we can't ship the whole lot at one time.

D: Why? Is there anything wrong with my order?

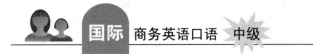

W: As far as your order is concerned, everything is all right. Only it's difficult for us to get all these 50,000 yards of cloth prepared within such a short period. So I propose partial shipment be allowed.

D: But our customers are in urgent need of these goods. I still hope you ship the whole lot at one time.

W: Mr. Dandy, maybe you are not clear about my point yet. It is your own interests that we put forward such a proposal. If partial shipment is allowed, instead of waiting for the whole lot to get ready, we can ship whatever is ready to fill the urgent need of your end-users.

D: I see what you mean. In that case I agree to partial shipment. But could you explain that in more detail?

W: In September, we'll deliver 50% and the balance will be shipped in the following month.

D: But could you make it better? Say, 70% will be delivered in September?

W: We'll do what we can. When all of the details of the shipment are finished, I'll send you all of the shipping documents that you will need to get the shipment.

D: Thank you very much. This time, could you take extra care to review all of the details on the shipping documents?

W: Absolutely. I know there was a mistake last time, and it was our fault. I promise it won't happen again.

▶ Dialogue 3　Discussing the Delivery Time

Ms. White (W) and Mr. Zhong (Z) are discussing the time of delivery.

W: If I remember correctly, time of delivery is another point on which we differ, Mr. Zhong.

Z: Right. Let's go into details.

W: OK. I hope you can have these goods delivered before the end of September. We'd like them to be there in time for our Christmas sales.

Z: Christmas doesn't come until almost the end of the year, does it?

W: But, in the United States the Christmas season begins about a month before December 25.

Z: Well, I'm afraid it'll be difficult for us to advance the time of shipment. Our manufacturers are fully committed at the moment.

W: I hope you'll try to get them to step up production.

Z: As new orders keep pouring in, the workers are working three shifts to step up production.

W: If that's the case, there's nothing more to be said.

Z: I'm sorry.

W: What's your last word as to the date then?

Z: I said by the middle of October. This is the best we can promise.

W: All right. I'll take you at your word.

Z: Good. Let's call it a deal. We'll do our best to advance the shipment, but your L/C should be opened by early September.

W: I promise.

 **Dialogue 4** **Exchanging Ideas on Terms of Shipment**

Ms. Black (B) is exchanging ideas with Mr. Wang (W) on terms of shipment.

B: Good morning, Mr. Wang. I'm glad to have this opportunity to exchange ideas with you on terms of shipment. First, let's decide the time of delivery.

W: We can ship the goods in October.

B: That'll be too late. You know, this is our seasonal product, so we've got to market it before the end of September in order to keep up with the season. Can you do something to advance the shipment to August.

W: Well, I understand, but I'm afraid it is very difficult to make it in August because our manufacturers are fully committed at the moment.

B: Then when is the earliest we can expect the shipment?

W: According to the manufacturers' schedule, the earliest possible date of delivery would be the end of September.

B: Let me put it this way. We've agreed to do this deal on an FOB basis. That means even if you deliver the goods at the end of September, it will still take us another two or three weeks to go through the Customs to get the goods onto the market. Now if you could advance the delivery three weeks earlier, everything will be fine and we'll be able to make it.

W: I see. I'll get in touch with my manufacturer and make sure if they can deliver the goods at the beginning of September.

B: Thank you. You know, a timely delivery means a lot to us. If we place our goods on the market at a time when all other importers have sold theirs at profitable price, we shall lose out. So, if the goods can not be shipped at the beginning of September, we shall be compelled to purchase elsewhere and may have to countermand our order.

W: I hope it won't happen. We'll do what we can to meet your demand. As soon as I confirm the earliest shipment, I'll give you a call.

B: I really appreciate this.

Words and Expressions

logistics	*n.* 物流	delivery	*n.* 交货
fruition	*n.* 成就，实现	advance	*v.* 提前
optimize	*v.* 持乐观态度	commit	*v.* 使承担任务
prestige	*n.* 声誉，声望，威望，威信	work three shift	三班工作
		timely	*a.* 及时的
stimulate	*v.* 激励，鼓励	compel	*v.* 强迫，不得不
cardboard	*n.* 硬纸板	countermand	*v.* 改变（订货），取消（订货），撤回
partial shipment	分批装运		

Notes

1. 产品包装

产品包装，一般地说就是给生产的产品装箱、装盒、装袋、包裹、捆扎的事。产品包装，是消费者对产品的视觉体验，是产品个性的直接和主要传递者，是企业形象定位的直接表现。好的包装设计是企业创造利润的重要手段之一。策略定位准确、符合消费者心理的产品包装设计，能帮助企业在众多竞争品牌中脱颖而出，并使公司赢得了"可靠"的声誉。包装技术的发展趋势如下：① 制订和推行多种有关机械包装的标准，如外形尺寸、包装材料质量、包装箱强度、检验方法等。② 改进包装材料，如推广应用高强度的瓦楞纸箱；发展适用于软包装的复合材料和高性能的新型塑料薄膜。③ 加强机械产品的包装设计工作，根据产品的不同特性，如重量、刚性、精密度、耐振动、防潮湿等进行试验研究，确定包装材料、形式和方法。④ 采用新技术，如对小工具和精密零部件采用真空吸塑包装，在包装热封中利用热管提高封装质量和减少热量损耗；利用激光和光纤技术，识别包装产品和检测包装质量；利用电子计算机进行程序控制，提高包装作业的机械化自动化程度。

2. 货物运输

运输即实物分配，包括企业、销售商自身的运输、仓储、包装和搬运等活动。运输首先作为"第三利润源"而引起重视的，所谓第三利润源，是针对企业的利润来源而言的，企业第一利润源来自企业销售额的增加，第二利润源是生产成本（针对制造商而言）或者进货成本（针对流通商而言）的降低，而由降低成本所得的利润则成为企业第三利润源。在这里，运输被定义为对物资的流通配置，包括制造商、流通商的装卸、运输、仓储、搬运等一系列的过程，对货运的重视被提高到降低成本、增加利润的高度，成为货运定义的第一个转折。

3. 交货

在买卖合同中，交货是指货物在交易双方之间的转移，即由卖方将货物转交给买方。其内容包括：交货地点、交货方式和交货时间。交货时间一般是规定一个期限，而不是某个具体日期。目前常用的有以下几种规定方法：① 规定在某月内装运；② 规定在某月月底以前装运；③ 规定在某月某日以前装运；④ 跨月装运，即规定在某两个月，三个月或几个月内装运；⑤ 规定在收到信用证后一定时间内运，一般还应同时规定开立信用证的期限；⑥ 在买方急需而卖方又备有现货的情况下，可采用近期交货术语作为交货时间。规定交货时间必须恰当可行，一般应结合下列情况考虑决定：① 货源情况；② 运输情况；③ 市场情况；④ 商品情况。

4. FOB

即 free on board，离岸价，指货物上船前的所有费用由卖方承担。

Useful Sentences

1. He should fall into love with your product at the first sight.
   应该能让他一眼就喜欢上你的产品。

2. You can say that again.
   您说得很对。/我很同意您的说法。

3. We'll do our best to suit children's taste.
   我们会尽力去适应孩子们的趣味。

4. Now let's have a short rest before we go on to the next point, shall we?
   在讨论下一个问题前，我们先休息一会儿好吗？

5. Mr. Dandy, I'm afraid we can't ship the whole lot at one time.
   丹迪先生，恐怕我们不能一次装运整批货物。

6. So I propose partial shipment be allowed.
   因此我建议分批装运。

7. It's your own interests that we put forward such a proposal.

我们提出这一建议正是为了你方的利益。

8. If partial shipment is allowed, instead of waiting for the whole lot to get ready, we can ship whatever is ready to fill the urgent need of your end-users.

如果允许分批装运，我们就可以装运现有的货物，以满足你方用户的急需，而不必等到全部货物备妥之后才装运。

9. This time, could you take extra care to review all of the details on the shipping documents?

这次您能不能多费心，把出口文件的所有细节都仔细检查一遍？

10. Let's go into details.

我们来详细谈谈吧。

11. Our manufacturers are fully committed at the moment.

我们厂家现已承约过多。

12. As new orders keep pouring in, the workers are working three shifts to step up production.

由于新的订单源源不断，工人们三班工作来加快生产。

13. All right. I'll take you at your word.

好吧，我就按您说的吧。

14. Then when is the earliest we can expect the shipment?

那最早能什么时候装船？

15. Let's put it this way. We've agreed to do this deal on an FOB basis.

我们这样说吧，我方已经同意以离岸价格来做这桩生意。

16. So, if the goods can not be shipped at the beginning of September, we shall be compelled to purchase eslewhere and may have to coutermand our order.

因此，如果货物不能在 9 月初装运，我们不得不向他处购买，可能得撤销订单。

Exercises

I Complete the following dialogues.

1. **A:** _____.

   （惹眼的包装自然会起到促销的作用。）

   B: You said it. We'll see to it.

2. **A:** Well, I'll fax home immediately for instructions on this matter.

   B: _____.

   （好的，我等着您的回音。）

3. **A:** _____.

   （你方最好将货物一次全部装运。）

   B: OK, we'll try our best to meet your demand.

4. **A:** How shall we deal with the transport charges?

   B: _____.

   （所有的运输费用都包括在到岸价中。）

5. **A:** _____.

   （由香港转船的要求可以接受。）

   B: You can say that again.

II Situational practice.

Make dialogues according to the following situations.

1. Imagine you are discussing the shipping date with your business partner, Mr. Green, who is planning to order electronic toys from your company. You both hold different ideas about the date of shipment. So you have to discuss with your business partner.

2. You are discussing tea packing with your business partner, Mr. White. And Mr. White proposes you should make some changes in packing.

对话汉译

▶ 对话 1　关于改善包装的建议

格林女士（G）参观了玩具厂，然后就产品包装问题与供货商徐先生（X）进行了商讨。

G: 徐先生，参观了你们的工厂后，我对你们的生产条件十分满意。

X: 嗯，那是我们主要的玩具出口基地，具有良好的生产经验和悠久的历史。我们的产品在国际市场上享有很高的声誉。

G: 你们的产品很好，这是毫无疑问的。不过，你们的包装需要改进。我可以给您提点建议吗？

X: 好的，您请讲。

G: 我们双方都知道包装的一项重要功能就是刺激顾客的购买欲望，应该能让他一眼就喜欢上你的产品。

X: 您说得很对。不过，您能说得再具体点吗？

G: 事实上，先用塑料袋进行包装，然后再装入图案精美、色彩鲜艳的纸盒的玩具在我方市场最畅销。你们的包装图案不错，但希望在色彩方面再做些改善。孩子们喜欢鲜艳的颜色。这就是我们对包装的建议。

X: 的确是个好主意。我们会尽力去适应孩子们的趣味。我将把您的建议转达给生产商，让他们进行改进。希望新的包装能更好地满足您的要求。

G: 但愿如此。那么关于外包装，你们打算怎样处理呢？

X: 喔，我们将用打包带从外面将所有的纸箱加固，并标上诸如"小心轻放"及其他用于运输的一般标志。

G: 不错。顺便问一句，你们接受中性包装吗？

X: 是的，我们可以根据你方授意来包装货物。您还有其他的有关包装的问题或要求吗？

G: 没有了，徐先生。

X: 在讨论下一个问题前，我们先休息一会儿好吗？

G: 好啊。

X: 请喝杯咖啡吧。

G: 谢谢。

▶ **对话 2 就装运问题进行磋商**

丹迪先生（D）打算一次装运整批货物，但是王女士（W）建议分批装运。

W: 丹迪先生，恐怕我们不能一次装运整批货物。

D: 为什么？我的订单有什么问题吗？

W: 就你们的订单而言，没问题。只不过我们很难在这么短的时间内装运好 50 000 码布。因此我建议分批装运。

D: 但我们的客户急需这批货。我还是希望你们能一次性装运整批货物。

W: 丹迪先生，可能你还没明白我的意思。我们提出这一建议正是为了您的利益。如果允许分批装运，我们就可以装运已有的货物，以满足你方用户的急需，而不必等到全部货物备妥之后才装运。

D: 我明白你的意思了。如果是那样，我同意分批装运，不过您能否更详细地说明一下？

W: 9 月份装运 50%，其余的后一个月交货。

D: 能不能再多一些呢？比如说，9 月份装运 70%。

W: 我们会尽力的。我把装运的所有细节完成后，就会把提货所需的货运单据全部寄给你。

D: 真是太谢谢您了。这次您能不能多费心，把出口文件的所有细节都仔细检查一遍？

W: 一定。我知道上次的文件有个地方弄错了，是我们的错，我保证这种事情绝对不会再发生。

▶ 对话 3   就交货时间进行磋商

怀特先生（W）正在和钟先生（Z）商讨交货的时间。

W: 钟先生，如果我没记错的话，交货时间是另一个我们有分歧的地方。

Z: 对。我们来详细谈谈吧。

W: 好的。我希望你方能在 9 月底之前交货。我们想让这批货赶上圣诞节销售。

Z: 圣诞节几乎就是年底了，对吗？

W: 但在美国，圣诞节大约在 12 月 25 日前一个月就开始了。

Z: 嗯，恐怕我方难以提前装船。我方厂家现已承约过多。

W: 希望你们尽力使厂家加快生产。

Z: 由于新的订单源源不断，工人们三班工作来加快生产。

W: 如果这样，那就没有什么可说的了。

Z: 很抱歉。

W: 那么，你方最后确定的装船日期是何时？

Z: 我说过是到 10 月中旬。这是我方所能做出的最佳允诺。

W: 好吧，我就按您说的吧。

Z: 好。我们成交吧。我方会尽力提前装船，但是你方的信用证应该在 9 月初开立。

W: 没问题。

▶ 对话 4   就装船事宜进行磋商

布莱克女士（B）和王先生（W）正在就装船事宜进行磋商。

B: 早上好，王先生。非常高兴能有这次机会和您一起交换一下有关装运的意见。首先让我们来定一下交货期。

W: 我们可以在 10 月装运货物。

B: 那就太迟了。这是季节性产品，因此为了能赶上季节，我们必须在 9 月底之前将产品投放市场。您能设法将装运提前到 8 月吗？

W: 喔，我懂，不过恐怕很难在 8 月办好，因为我们的厂商目前已承约太多。

B: 那最早能什么时候装船？

W: 按照厂商的日程安排，最早的交货期可能是 9 月底。

B: 我这样说吧，我方已经同意以离岸价格来做这桩生意。这就意味着即使你方在 9 月底交货，我方仍需花两到三周的时间才能通过海关将货物投放市场。你方只要提前三周发货，事情就办好了，我们就能赶上销售季节。

W: 我明白了。我会与厂商联系，看看他们是否能在 9 月初发货。

B: 谢谢。您知道，适时交货对我们来说十分重要。如果其他的进口商在我们之前把他们的商品以好价钱售出，那我们就亏本了。因此，如果货物不能在 9 月初装运，我们不得不向他处购买，可能得撤销订单。

W: 希望这种事不要发生。我们会尽力满足你方要求。最早装运期一经确定，我就立即给您打电话。

B: 非常感谢。

Extended Reading

Production Logistics

The term "production logistics" is used to describe logistic processes within an industry. The purpose of production logistics is to ensure that each machine and workstation is being fed with the right product in the right quantity and quality at the right time. The concern is not the transportation itself, but to streamline and control the flow through value-adding processes and eliminate non-value-adding ones. Production logistics can be applied to existing as well as new plants. Manufacturing in an existing plant is a constantly changing process. Machines are exchanged and new ones added, which gives the opportunity to improve the production logistics system accordingly. Production logistics provides the means to achieve customer response and capital efficiency.

Production logistics is becoming more important with decreasing batch sizes. In many industries (e.g. mobile phones), a batch size of one is the short-term aim, allowing even a single customer's demand to be fulfilled efficiently. Track and tracing, which is an essential part of production logistics — due to product safety and product reliability issues — is also gaining importance, especially in the automotive and medical industries.

Topic discussion:

1. What is the importance of logistics in international business?
2. What factors should be included in doing the business logistics?

其他常用词汇和短语

appearance *n.* 外观，外表

background *n.* 底色

bar code 条形码

catch the eye 引人注目

dampness *n.* 受潮，潮湿

dealer (distributor) *n.* 经销商

desirable *a.* 称心如意的

dispatch money and demurrage 速遣费与滞期费

distinctive *a.* 独特的

exquisite *a.* 优美的，高雅的，精巧的，精致的

fragile *a.* 易碎的，易损坏的

freight *n.* 货运，运费

freight cost 运输成本

freight forwarder 运输公司，转运公司

freight paid in advance 预付运费

freighter *n.* 承运人，货船

gross weight 毛重

handling *n.* 装卸，操纵

illustration *n.* 插图，说明，图解

indicative mark 指示性标志

international inter-modal/multimodal/combined transport 国际联运

liner transport 班轮运输

lorry *n.* 运货汽车，卡车

metal strap 金属带

mode of transport 运输方式

net weight 净重

non-negotiable *a.* 不能议付的，非流通的

notice of readiness (N/R) 装卸准备就绪通知书

novel *a.* 新颖的，新奇的

ocean freight 海运运费

promote *v.* 宣传，推销

promoting the sales 促销

recognizable *a.* 可辨认的，可认出的

seaworthy *a.* 适于航海的，经得起风浪的

shipping by chartering 租船运输

spoil *v.* 损坏

stand *v.* 经受得住

strengthen *v.* 加固，使牢固

time charter 定期租船

trademark *n.* 商标

transit *n.* 运输

transparent *a.* 透明的

transshipment to be allowed 可以转船运输

voyage charter 航次运输，程租船

warning mark 警示标志

waterproof paper 防水纸

wrapper *n.* 包装物

Unit

8

Business Insurance
商 业 保 险

Learning Resources

Dialogues

▶ **Dialogue 1** **Talking about the Insurance of Ocean Marine Cargo**

Mr. Zhang (Z) enters an insurance company and talks with its manager (M) about the insurance of ocean marine cargo.

M: What kind of insurance policy would you like? I'm sure we can help you in any way you need.

Z: We'll have a shipment from the United States. We want to find out your marine insurance.

M: Well, since you told me the goods are very important, I think insurance against all risks is the broadest kind of standard coverage.

Z: I know that. But I don't think there is any chance that our goods will be stolen, for example, so I think we don't need a policy that is so expensive.

M: May I suggest a free from particular average (FPA) policy? That will cover you if the ship sinks or burns, or gets stuck.

Z: That's better, but I think we need to cover more kinds of things, like damage by sea water, for example.

M: How about with particular average (WPA) policy? It covers more risks than the FPA. It covers you against partial loss in all cases.

Z: That's a good idea. I have one more question here. How long is the period from the commencement to termination of insurance?

M: The cover shall be limited to sixty days upon discharge of the insured goods from the seagoing vessel at the final port of discharge.

Z: By the way, in the event of loss or of damage to my goods, what is the procedure for filing a claim?

M: If any loss or damage occurs, you may lodge a claim with their agent at your port. The claim is to be supported by a survey report and put in within 60 days after the arrival of the consignment. In the light of the actual findings, they'll compensate you for the loss according to the provisions of the insurance policy.

Z: Thank you very much. You've answered many questions about insurance for me.

M: You're welcome. Come back if you have any questions, OK?

Z: OK. See you.

M: See you.

 **Dialogue 2**   **Talking about Questions on Business Insurance**

Mr. Black (B) asks Ms. Chen (C) to explain to him a few questions on business insurance.

B: Ms. Chen, I have a few questions on insurance and would be grateful if you could explain them to me.

C: Sure. I'll try my best to help.

B: Now, suppose we will pay the price you offered for the goods, how will the goods be insured?

C: We will insure the goods against loading damage and transportation. That is, we insure the safe arrival of the goods in the sea port you specify, but certainly it will not include the unloading damage.

B: Could you explain the transportation insurance coverage?

C: Sure. The transportation insurance here refers to free from particular average. We call it WPA.

B: Does it cover any damage caused by natural disasters and accidents?

C: Generally speaking, it does.

B: How about theft, breakage and rain water damage?

C: I'm afraid not. I mean you don't need that. They are not delicate goods. They are not likely to get these kinds of damage.

B: You are probably right. Could you tell me a general sum of money for WPA?

C: Well, about $50 a ton.

B: I see. I think I need to discuss the matter with my boss before I tell you our final decision.

C: Sure. You could send us an e-mail or fax, or simply give us a call, if you have any questions about it. All right?

B: Yes. No problem. Thank you very much for your explanations.

▶ Dialogue 3   Talking about the Insurance in the Contract

Mr. Johnson (J) and Ms. Li (L) are talking about some problems about insurance involved in their contract.

J: We would like to ask you some details about this agreement. Have you taken out insurance yet on this shipment?

L: Yes. We talked about it with our underwriter, and think that we should get a policy for with particular average, considering our deal is based on CIF clause. Is there anything you would like to know or…

J: No. Not really. I was just wondering if the breakage of goods is included in this WPA or not. You know, this consignment is easy to be broken.

L: In fact, not every breakage is included in this WPA. It is included in the WPA when the breakage is resulted from natural calamities and maritime accidents, such as stranding and sinking of the carrying vessel, or is attributable to fire, explosion or collision. Or else it belongs to the risk of breakage. We could add this item if you wish.

J: But that's an additional risk item, isn't it?

L: Yes. And the buyer is usually required to bear the cost for the additional risk coverage.

J: I see. What if we change to all risks? Do we still have to pay extra for the risk of breakage?

L: No, you don't have to. The insurance of All Risks has that item under coverage already. However, all you need to do is to pay a little higher premium rate.

J: That really doesn't matter. The value of the goods is just too high. If we lose them our company will lose a lot of money, and may have to close. So the safety of the goods is all that counts.

L: Oh, yes, absolutely. I'll have your insurance changed from WPA to all risks for 110% of CIF invoice value as per the ocean marine cargo clause of the PICC.

J: Very good. Another thing, what about the scope of the insurance coverage? I mean, where does it start and where does it end?

L: We adopt the warehouse to warehouse clause which is commonly used in international insurance. In other words, the coverage is in effect when the cargo has left the consigner's warehouse and all the through transit to the consignee's warehouse.

J: I see. Thank you for your cooperation.

L: It's my pleasure.

▶ **Dialogue 4** **Choosing Proper Business Insurance**

Miss Green (G) is discussing with Mr. Huang (H) over the proper choice of business insurance.

G: Mr. Huang, I'd like to have a talk with you over the question of insurance, if you don't mind.

H: No. Not a bit. Go ahead, please.

G: What kind of insurance is PICC able to provide for my consignment?

H: PICC can provide a broad range of coverage against all kinds of risks for sea transport, such as free from particular average, with particular average, all risks and extraneous risks. But what coverage you will take out should be suitable for your goods.

G: If we conclude the business on CIF basis, what coverage will you take out for the goods?

H: Generally speaking, we only insure the goods WPA.

G: Do you cover risks other than WPA, for instance, TPND (theft, pilferage and non-delivery), fresh or rainwater damage, risk of shortage, leakage risk, clashing and breakage risk and so on?

H: Yes. But these risks belong to extraneous risks. According to the international practice, we do not insure against such risks unless they are called for by the buyers. And it is the buyer who will pay for the extra premium.

G: I see. Now could you let me know how to calculate the insurance premium?

H: The premium is to be calculated in this way. First, find out the premium rate for the goods, that is x%, and second, consider what risks are covered. Then calculate the total value you are insuring. Usually we cover the insurance for 110% of the invoice value.

G: Can I have the goods insured for 130% of the invoice value?

H: Yes, but please note that the extra premium for the difference between 130% and 110% should be borne by the buyer.

G: That's understood. Thank you very much.

H: You're welcome.

Words and Expressions

hedge *v.* 规避，避免	commencement *n.* 开始，开端
contingent *n.* 偶然，意外	termination *n.* 终点，终止，结束
equitable *a.* 公平的，公正的，合理的	consignment *n.* 交付，委托
entity *n.* 实体	massage *n./v.* 按摩，推拿
policyholder *n.* 被保险人	breakage *n.* 破坏，毁损，断裂
policy *n.* 保险单	underwriter *n.* 保险，（特指）水险商
premium *n.* 保险费	calamity *n.* 灾难，灾害
discrete *a.* 分离的，分立的	strand *v.* 使（船等）触礁，使搁浅
indemnify *v.* 补偿，赔偿	attributable *a.* 可归因于……的，由……引起的
devastating *a.* 毁灭性的	collision *n.* 碰撞
marine *a.* 海的，海上的，海事的，海运的	scope *n.* 范围
	warehouse *n.* 仓库，货栈

Notes

1. 商业保险

所有有经验的出口商都知道运输货物时存在风险。这包括火灾、暴风雨、装卸损坏、盗窃、渗漏和爆炸等。必须为运送到另一个国家的货物在运输过程中可能出现的丢失或损坏等风险购买保险。这样一来，不论采用什么样的运输方式，出口商和进口商都不会遭受任何损失。

保险有三个主要原则：第一，可保权益原则，指一个人只有在一件事情中拥有利益才能投保；第二，最大诚信原则，指确定保费的人们根据提交申请表的书面声明，决定某项保险的保费是否合理；第三，赔偿原则，认为保险合同只将受益人的利益恢复到发生损害之前的同等状况。

保险对确保国际贸易中货物的安全发挥着重要作用。保险公司承保的货运保险涵盖从一个国家到另一个国家运输过程中所产生的损失。货运保险单实质上是一份承保人和被保险人之间的合同，它规定了保费、投保或没有投保的险种、理赔的程序以及所有其他可适用的条款。

2. 平安险（free from particular average，FPA）

这一名称在我国保险行业中沿用甚久，其英文原意是指单独海损不负责赔偿。根据国际保险界对单独海损的解释，它是指保险标的物在海上运输途中遭受保险范围内的风险直接造成的船舶或货物的灭失或损害。因此，平安险的原来保障范围只赔全部损失。但在长期实践的过程中对平安险的责任范围进行了补充和修订，当前平安险的责任范围已经超出只赔全损的限制。

3. 水渍险（with particular average，WPA）

又称"单独海损险"，英文原意是指单独海损负责赔偿，海洋运输货物保险的主要险别之一。水渍险的责任范围除了包括上列"平安险"的各项责任外，还负责被保险货物由于恶劣气候、雷电、海啸、地震、洪水等自然灾害所造成的部分损失。 具体来说还分为是海水浸渍还是雨水浸渍。有的是不赔雨水浸渍的。就算有水浸渍，还要看那水是引起的货物损害的直接原因还是间接原因。是间接原因的话，保险公司是不赔的。

4. 一切险或综合险（all risks）

责任范围除包括上列水渍险的所有责任外，还包括货物在运输过程中，因一般外来风险所造成保险货物的损失。如被窃、雨淋、渗漏、碰损、破碎、串味、受潮受热、钩损等。不论全损或部分损失，除对某些运输途耗的货物，经保险公司与被保险人双约定在保险单上载明的免赔率外，保险公司都给予赔偿。

Useful Sentences

1. By the way, in the event of loss or of damage to my goods, what is the procedure for filing a claim?

   顺便问一句，如果货物丢失或受损，该如何提出索赔？

2. In the light of the actual findings, they'll compensate you for the loss according to the provisions of the insurance policy.

根据实际调查的结果，他们会按保险条款对你方进行赔偿。

3. That is, we insure the safe arrival of the goods in the sea port you specify, but certainly it will not include the unloading damage.

即我们保障货物安全抵达您指定的海港，当然该保险不包括卸货所致的损害。

4. It is included in the WPA when the breakage is resulted from natural calamities and maritime accidents, such as stranding and sinking of the carrying vessel, or is attributable to fire, explosion or collision.

只有因自然灾害及海上意外事故而造成的破损，如货船搁浅、沉没，或由于火灾、爆炸或碰撞所引起的破损才属于水渍险的范围。

5. In other words, the coverage is in effect when the cargo has left the consigner's warehouse and all the through transit to the consignee's warehouse.

也就是说，当货物离开发货人的仓库时，保险即开始生效，直至运输全程结束并当货物抵达收货人的仓库为止。

6. Mr. Huang, I'd like to have a talk with you over the question of insurance, if you don't mind.

黄先生，如果您不介意，我想跟您谈谈保险的问题。

7. If we conclude the business on CIF basis, what coverage will you take out for the goods?

如果我们的这批货物以到岸价格成交的话，你们会负责投保哪些险别？

8. And it is the buyer who will pay for the extra premium.

并且额外的保险费由买方支付。

Exercises

I **Complete the following dialogues.**

1. **A:** _____.

  （你们准备为我们这批货保什么险呢？）

  B: Usually we'll only insure WPA for this kind.

2. **A:** But that's an additional risk item, isn't it?

  B: _____.

  （对，并且通常都要由买方承担附加险的费用。）

3. **A:** _____?

  （您好，魏先生派我来与您谈谈保险的事，可以吗？）

  B: Yes, of course.

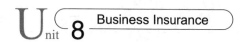

4. **A:** Should the insurance document be issued as a certificate?

   B: _____.

   （应该签发为保险证，因为这是信用证上明确规定的。）

5. **A:** _____?

   （您能否解释一下运输保险范围？）

   B: Sure. The transportation insurance here refers to free particular average. We call it WPA.

II Situational practice.

Make dialogues according to the following situations.

1. Imagine you are discussing with your business partner Mr. White about your ocean marine cargo, how do you better insure your cargo against some potential risks?

2. You are doing business with Mr. Black, and you hold different ideas on the choice of insurance coverage, what measures will you take to make two parties reach agreement.

对话汉译

▶ 对话 1 洽谈海运货物保险事宜

张先生（Z）走入保险公司并与其经理（M）洽谈海运货物保险事宜。

M: 您想投保哪一种险别？我们肯定可以提供您所需要的任何服务。

Z: 我们有一批要从美国装运的货物。我想了解一下你们的海上保险情况。

M: 嗯，既然您说这批货很重要，我想投综合险是最好的。

Z: 我也知道综合险是保险范围最广的险种。但是，举个例子，我想我们的货物不可能被偷，所以我认为我们不需要这么贵的保险。

M: 平安险怎么样？如果船沉了、烧毁了或搁浅了，您都会得到赔偿的。

Z: 这个好一些，不过我想我们需要再多涵盖一些内容，例如水渍损害之类。

M: 水渍险怎么样？它比平安险所覆盖的范围要广。在任何情况下，它都为您的部分损失保险。

Z: 这个不错。我还有一个问题，保险责任的期限是多长？

M: 被保险的货物在即货港卸离海轮之后，保险责任以 60 天为限。

Z: 顺便问一句，如果货物丢失或受损，该如何提出索赔？

M: 如果发生任何损失或损坏，您可在你方港口向保险公司代理商提出索赔。索赔须由检验报告证实，并且在货物运抵后 60 天内提出。根据实际调查的结果，他们会按保险条款对你方进行赔偿。

Z: 谢谢您。您已回答了我许多有关保险的问题。

M: 不必客气。如果您有什么问题请再来，好吗？

Z: 好的，再见。

M: 再见。

▶ 对话 2　谈论商业保险方面的问题

布莱克先生（B）向陈女士（C）请教一些商业保险方面的问题。

B: 陈女士，我有几个保险方面的问题，如果您能给我解释一下，我将不胜感激。

C: 好的。我会尽力的。

B: 嗯，假如我们愿意支付您的货款的话，货物会得到怎样的保险呢？

C: 我们为货物的装载和运输进行投保。即我们保障货物安全抵达您指定的海港，但是该保险不包括卸货所致的损害。

B: 您能否解释一下运输保险范围？

C: 可以。这里的运输保险指的是平安险。我们称之为 WPA。

B: 它包括自然灾害和意外事故造成的损失吗？

C: 一般来说是包括的。

B: 是否包括偷窃、破损和雨淋损失？

C: 恐怕不包括。我是说你们不需要这种保险，它们不是精细货物，它们不可能遭到这些损害。

B: 您或许说得对。能不能给我说一说平安险的大概保险费？

C: 嗯，大概每吨 50 美元。

B: 知道了，我想我需要和我们的老板商量后才能做决定。

C: 当然。如果有什么问题的话，你们可以给我们发电子邮件或传真，或直接打电话。行吗？

B: 好的，没问题，谢谢您耐心的解释。

▶ 对话 3　商谈合同中的保险问题

约翰逊先生（J）正与李女士（L）商谈合同中的保险问题。

J: 我们想请教您有关这份协议书的一些细节问题。你方是否已经为这批货物投保了？

L: 是的，我们跟保险商商谈过了。考虑到这笔生意是以到岸价格条件成交的，我们认为应该投保水渍险。还有什么不清楚的地方吗，或者……

J: 没有。我只是在想货物的破损是否也包括在水渍险中。您知道这批货容易破损。

L: 事实上，并非所有的破损都包括在水渍险中。只有因自然灾害及海上意外事故而造成的破损，如货船搁浅、沉没，或由于着火灾、爆炸或碰撞所引起的破损才属于水渍险的范围。否则，就属于破损险。如果您需要，我们可以加上此项。

J: 但那属于附加险，对吗？

L: 对，并且通常都要由买方承担这笔额外的保险费。

J: 我明白了。如果我们换成综合险呢？还会要求我们负担破损险这一额外费用吗？

L: 那就不必了。破损险已包含在综合险的范围之内。您只需要支付稍高一点的保险费率。

J: 那倒没有关系。这批货物价值不菲，如果弄丢了，公司会亏损很多钱，还有可能因此倒闭呢！所以货物的安全是非常重要的。

L: 喔，是的，这绝对重要。我会将水渍险改成综合险，根据中国人民保险公司海洋货物运输条例，按到岸价发票金额的 110% 进行投保。

J: 很好。另外，保险范围是怎样的呢？我的意思是从哪里算起，又从哪里结束？

L: 我们采用国际保险中惯用的货仓到货仓的责任条款。也就是说，当货物离开发货人的仓库时，保险即开始生效，直至运输全程结束并当货物抵达收货人的仓库为止。

J: 明白了。谢谢您的合作。

L: 别客气。

> ▶ **对话 4** 如何选择合适的商业保险

格林小姐（G）正在与黄先生（H）商量选择一种合适的保险。

G: 黄先生，如果您不介意，我想跟您谈谈保险的问题。

H: 没问题，您请讲。

G: 中国人民保险公司可以为我的货物提供何种险别的保险？

H: 中国人民保险公司可以承担海洋运输的所有险别，例如：平安险、水渍险、一切险，以及附加险。但是，您所选择投保的险别必须适合于您的货物。

G: 如果我们的这批货物以到岸价格成交的话，你们会负责投保哪些险别？

H: 一般来说，我们只投保水渍险。

G: 除了水渍险外，你们还投保其他险别吗？比如：偷窃、提货不着险，淡水雨淋险，短重险，渗漏险，碰损、破损险等。

H: 可以投保。但这些险别属于附加险。按照国际惯例除非买方要求，我们通常不投保这些险别，并且额外的保险费由买方支付。

G: 我明白了。那您能告诉我如何计算保险费吗？

H: 保险费是这样计算的：首先，要查看这种货物的保险费率，即 x%，第二步，要看您所投保的险别。然后按照您所投保的总价值来计算。我们通常是按照发票金额的110%来投保的。

G: 我可以按发票金额的130%来投保吗？

H: 可以，但请注意，130%与110%之间的差额所引起的额外保险费应由买方支付。

G: 明白了，非常感谢。

H: 不客气。

Extended Reading

Types of Insurance

Any risk that can be quantified can potentially be insured. Specific kinds of risk that may give rise to claims are known as "perils". An insurance policy will set out in details which perils are covered by the policy, and which are not. Below are (non-exhaustive) lists of the many different types of insurance that exist. A single policy may cover risks in one or more of the categories set out below. For example, auto insurance would typically cover both property risk (covering the risk of theft or damage to the car) and liability risk (covering legal claims from causing an accident). A homeowner's insurance policy in the U.S. typically includes property insurance covering damage to the home and the owner's belongings, liability insurance covering certain legal claims against the owner, and even a small amount of coverage for medical expenses of guests who are injured on the owner's property.

Business insurance can be any kind of insurance that protects businesses against risks. Some principal subtypes of business insurance are (a) the various kinds of professional liability insurance, also called professional indemnity insurance, which are discussed below under that name; and (b) the business owner's policy (BOP), which bundles into one policy many of the kinds of coverage that a business owner needs, in a way analogous to how homeowners insurance bundles the coverage that a homeowner needs.

Topic discussion:

1. What has the insurance brought for you?

2. What role does insurance play in international business?

其他常用词汇和短语

actual total loss　实际全损

air transportation insurance　航空运输保险

all risks　综合险，一切险

arbitration　n.　仲裁

arrange/cover/effect/provide/take out insurance　投保，洽办保险

bindng　a.　有约束力的，附有义务的

bureau　n.　局，处，所

certificate of quality　质量证明书

certificate of weight　重量证明书

clashing and breakage risk　碰损、破碎险

compensate　v.　赔偿

comprehensively　ad.　全面地，彻底地

constructive total loss　推定全损

delicate goods　易损易碎的货物

discrepency　n.　差异

dispute　n.　纠纷，争执

disqualification　n.　不合格

explosion　n.　爆炸

extraneous risks　附加险

free from particular average (FPA)　平安险

fresh or rainwater damage　淡水雨淋险

general average (GA)　共同海损

inspection　n.　检验

Institue Cargo Clauses (ICC)　（伦敦保险协会的）协会货物保险条款

insurance　n.　保险

insurance amount　保险额

insurance certificate　保险凭证

insurance coverage　保险范围

insurance policy　保险单，投保单

insurance rate　保险费率

insurer　n.　保险人，承保人

intantaneously　ad.　瞬间地，即刻地

involve　v.　牵涉，包含

leakage risk　渗漏险

marine insurance　海运险

marine perils and losses　海上风险与损失

marine policy　海运保险单

natural calamities　自然灾害

ocean marine cargo insurance　海运货物保险

overland insurance　陆上险

parcel post insurance　邮包险

performance　n.　性能，表现

release　v. & n.　释放，放行

responsibility　n.　责任

risk to shortweight (shortweight risk)　短重险

shortweight　n.　短重

sinking　n.　沉没

stranding　n.　搁浅

strikes, riot and civil commotion (SRCC)　罢工、暴动、民变险

submit　v.　提交，提出

survey report　调查报告

sweating and heating risks　受潮受热险

taint of odour risk　串味险

theft, pilferage and non-delivery (TPND)
　偷窃提货不着险

undertake　*v.* 承担，从事

veterinary inspection certificate　动物
　检疫证明

war risk　兵险（战争险）

with particular average（WPA）水渍险
　（单独海损险）

Unit

9

Complaints and Reply on Product and Service

对产品与服务的投诉及受理

Learning Resources

Claim letters are very important in any business. Writing claim letters are both a Science and an Art. There are obviously many different ways to write claim letters, but the ideal approach for your case depends on condition and situation.

Selecting the best words is very important in writing an effective claim letter.

Always remember claim letter is not the place to try out fancy fonts or experimental writing styles. When writing claim letters, you should make sure to double check your claim letter for finding and correcting grammar and spelling mistakes. So remember to proofread your claim letter.

Dialogues

 **Dialogue 1** **Complaining about the Quality of Goods**

Mr. Byron (B) complains about underweight and inferior quality of his import products to Ms. Feng (F) and lodges a claim.

B: Good morning, Ms. Feng. This is Jack Byron from an Australian Import and Export Company.

F: Good morning, Mr. Byron. What can I do for you?

B: I have something very unpleasant to talk over with you, Ms. Feng.

F: Go ahead, please.

B: The goods you sent to us are not in conformity with the specifications of the contract and made us lose a lot of money, so we feel that you should fix up the problems and make it up to us.

F: Just be patient, please. Any criticism on our goods is sincerely invited. Let's talk about the problems first.

B: As soon as the shipment arrived at our port, we had it inspected. To our disappointment, we found the goods were underweight.

F: Is that so? OK, I'll check why the goods were underweight.

B: Good. As well, we feel that the percentage of the goods of inferior quality was too high.

F: I'm sorry you feel like that. As everybody knows, our products enjoy high prestige in the world. Complaints about our quality are very rare indeed. But I promise I'll check into these problems, and find out if they were our fault.

B: OK. I'll be waiting for your result.

(Several days later)

F: Good afternoon, Mr. Byron. This is Feng Ying speaking.

B: Good afternoon, Ms. Feng. Glad to hear your voice. Have you found out the causes of the problems?

F: Yes. As to the underweight, I'd like to point out that the goods were weighted before shipment. The certificate confirms we delivered full shipment weight. So I think the shortage might have occurred during transit. Therefore, your claim, in my opinion, should be referred to insurance company as the liability rests with them.

B: Then, how about the inferior quality?

F: Upon investigation, we have found that the error occurred in the factory. Some of the workers mistook Article No. 103 for No. 102 when they packed the goods. The two articles are of different grade. We're really sorry for that and we'd like to accept your claim on it. Please tell us what you want us to do.

B: You can make amends for the losses by replacing all of the inferior products, and paying for the business we have lost.

F: That sounds OK. One of my people will go to your company tomorrow and talk about what replacements are needed, and the money for your other losses.

B: I really appreciate your correct attitude in this case. And I sincerely hope that everything will be smooth in our future business.

F: Please believe me this is a singular case. I'm sure that everything will be smooth in our future business.

▶ Dialogue 2 Discussing the Details of Claim

Mr. Zhu (Z) and Ms. Cade (C) are talking about the details of the claim.

Z: I'm glad you come here, Ms. Cade.

C: Nice to see you, Mr. Zhu. I'm here to investigate the matter of your claim for the breakage of the packages.

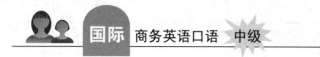

Z: Since we have sent you a notice of claim, I'm sure you know the details of our claim.

C: You said that nearly 25% of the packages had been broken.

Z: Yes. We think it was clearly due to improper packing.

C: I don't think so. Before I came here, I checked up on the condition of the shipment, and found nothing was wrong with the packing in our record. I think the breakage must have been caused by rough handling. Therefore I shall advise you to claim on the shipping company. You know, the goods were sold on FOB terms…

Z: Sorry to interrupt you, but according to the contract, no second-hand gunny bags are allowed to be used. To our regret, you used 280 second-hand ones. And poor packing was the cause of the damage and nothing else. If you had carried out the contract to the full, there would have been no damage at all. Why should we claim on the shipping company? How could we expect them to entertain our claim?

C: I beg your pardon? Are you sure that any second-hand bags are used for the last shipment?

Z: Sure enough! Here is the survey report issued by the China Commodity Inspection Bureau. You may read it.

C: *(After reading the survey report)* Can I have a look at the consignment?

Z: Yes, of course. They are still in the warehouse at the port, and we are waiting for your inspection. Let's go.

C: *(After seeing the broken packages in the warehouse)* How did it happen, I wonder? I really cannot stand the embarrassing mistake. Please accept my deepest apology for the problem.

Z: That's all right. But the repacking did take us a long time and the expenses amounted to RMB 5,000. We expect compensation for this amount and the inspection fee. I hope you'll consider our claim seriously.

C: Certainly. We should settle it according to the contract.

Z: I'm very glad to hear you say so. Thanks for your cooperation.

▶ Dialogue 3　Negotiating the Amount of Compensation

Miss. He (H) and Mr. James (J) are discussing how much compensation will be made.

H: Mr. James, if the case were not serious, I'd not come here to talk it over in person. Your bill of lading is found to be antedated. We wish you to give us a reasonable explanation.

J: I'm terribly sorry for what happened. Our consignment of goods was delayed for a couple of weeks. We have no choice but to antedate the B/L.

H: In our country such case is very serious.

J: Let me explain it. It was stipulated in the contract that the shipment date was on May 8th. However, the vessel reached the port on May 8th. It's impossible for us to finish loading and send the ship off on the same day.

H: No matter what reason it is. This transaction was concluded on CIF basis. Since you've been doing export business for years, you know who should be responsible for the shipment.

J: I'm sorry. We never expected that caused you so much trouble.

H: This is something done against the commercial conventions and laws concerned. You'd be prepared to pay the relevant compensation.

J: What's your requirement then?

H: 20% compensation must be made, no room for any concession.

J: That means 35,000 dollars for us. But we accept it anyway.

 **Dialogue 4** **Talking about the Responsiblity of Moldy Dried Vegetables and Compensation**

Ms. Zhao (Z) and Mr. Smith (S) are talking about who should be responsible for moldy dried vegetables and compensate for the loss.

Z: Mr. Smith, I'd like to talk with you about the quality of 100 cartons of dried vegetables. They reached us two weeks ago, and were immediately examined after they arrived. To our astonishment, about 10% of them were moldy. We can't accept them in this state.

S: Is that so? So far we haven't had any complaint of this kind. Have you got any evidence?

Z: Certainly. Here's survey report by a well-known lab in London.

S: There are many factors involved. What's more, your surveyors have not mentioned any cause for the damage.

Z: It is stated on the surveyor's report that extrinsic conditions of goods at the time of survey are all sound and intact. So it is obvious the cause of the damage is that the vegetables were not completely dried before packing.

S: As you know, before shipment, the Commodity Inspection Bureau inspected the goods and concluded that they were well-dehydrated from fresh and up to standard for export.

Z: I think the Inspection Bureau at your end, when effecting inspection, only selected a few packages at random, these happened to be up to the standard. As the amount in question is only 10% of the whole shipment, I think it is reasonable that you should compensate us for the loss.

S: The inspection certificate, which is based on a random selection of 10% of the consignment as we've agreed on beforehand, is considered final and binding upon both parties. Your claim, in our opinion, should be referred to the insurance company as the mishap occurred after shipment.

Z: We've already got in touch with the underwriter. But they have refused to accept any liability. They attributed the accident to the effects of dampness during the long sea voyage.

Words and Expressions

conformity   *n.*   相似,符合,适合,
　一致
specifications   *n.*   规范,规格
liability   *n.*   责任
amends   *n.*   赔偿,赎罪
singular   *a.*   唯一的,独一的,单
　独的,罕见的,异常的
gunny bags   黄麻袋
antedate   *v.*   把……上的日期填

早（若干时间）
stipulate   *v.*   约定,订立,规定,订明
vessel   *n.*   船
concession   *n.*   让步,迁就,让与
moldy   *a.*   发霉的
extrinsic   *a.*   外在的,非本质的
sound and intact   完整无缺
dehydrate   *v.*   脱水,失水

Notes

1. 短重投诉

当买方提出短重投诉时,卖方应注意,要正确使用计量单位。国际贸易中,现行的度量衡制度有公制、国际制、英制和美制。在这些度量衡制度进行过程中,要注意计量单位的正确使用。如遇买方进行数量索赔时,如属短交,卖方应看其是否在合同规定的溢短装范围之内,如在其范围之内,不属违约,只找差价就行了。同时买方也应注意,卖方如短交在 15% 以内,可要求卖方补交,或从货款中扣除相应的部分。

2. 货物损坏索赔

发现货物受到损坏要求索赔时,应该从事情的具体情况出发,本着平等互利和实事

求是的精神确定赔偿金额和其他处理方式，如退货、换货、补货、整修、延期付款、延期交货等。处理索赔的方法要尽量合情合理，以利于今后合作。解决索赔要求时，必须认真引证合同相关条款和证明文件的相关语句，要求对方出示必要的证明文字材料、实物材料、检验数据等，要详细核查，必要时要亲自到现场检验货物，眼见为实，方能决定赔偿的数额和方式。在买方提出索赔要求时，务必准备好所有必要的文件、证明和相关材料，有理有据。

3. 接受索赔

当客户提出投诉并要求索赔，公司内部必须细心应付，避免事件扩大，损及企业形象。再者，索赔事件若处理得当，不仅可以消除企业危机，甚至能够得到客户的谅解和长期支持。如果资金上难以承受的话，就和客人协商尽量少地赔偿。如果的确是自己的问题，想保住客户，则只能按照客户要求索赔了，从某种程度讲，这也维持了公司的信誉度。

4. 拒绝索赔

当对方提出索赔时，首先要弄清楚整件事的来龙去脉，然后弄清楚索赔是否理由充分。如果索赔理由充分，要向对方道歉，并尽量解决问题。如果索赔理由不充分，要礼貌含蓄地向对方做出解释，不管对方索赔的理由是否充分，但毕竟是公司的客户，他们的任何评论都会影响公司的声誉。如果不能马上着手处理这个问题，那么应向对方做出解释，并承诺会尽快采取行动。

Useful Sentences

1. Up to now, we haven't received the goods we ordered last month.
   我们至今还没有收到上个月订的货。

2. We have lost considerable business on account of your delay in delivering.
   由于贵方的延迟供货，我们已经丢掉了大笔的生意。

3. You should be responsible for all the losses resulting from the delayed delivering.
   贵方应对延误供货造成的一切损失负责。

4. The goods are not up to the standard stipulated in the contract. We're now lodging a claim with you.
   货不对板，所以我方提出索赔。

5. Your goods cannot be accepted as they differ from your samples.
   货不对板，所以我方拒绝接受这批货物。

6. Since it's our error, we'll pay the freight charges.

因为错误是我们造成的，我们会负担运费。

7. Would you mind waiting a few minutes while I check with my shipping department?

您可以稍等几分钟好让我和我们的货物运输部门核对一下吗？

8. I'm very pleased we were able to get to the bottom of this so quickly.

我很高兴能这么快把事情弄个水落石出。

9. Our customers reported that your products are very poor in quality.

我们的客户反映，你们的产品质量太差。

10. When unpacking the bales, we found that the materials are different from the original design.

我们拆开包裹后发现原料与原始设计不一致。

11. We shall be glad to have your explanation of this discrepancy in the quality, and also to know what you propose to do in the matter.

我们希望贵公司能对品质上的瑕疵加以说明，同时希望知道贵公司的处理办法。

12. We have examined the contents and found that 18 pieces were missing and the rest were unfit for use.

我们检查了所装货物，发现18件丢失，其余的无法使用。

13. We have to hold you responsible for the loss caused by the shortage.

我方因短重所造成的损失须由你方负责。

14. About 20% was found damaged on arrival.

到货时，发现有大约20%的货物受损。

15. Please return at our expense the goods you have received.

请将所收货物退回，运费由我方支付。

16. Here is a list of damaged items.

这是受损商品的清单。

17. After making a thorough investigation, we have decided to accept your claim and to compensate you the sum involved.

经过详细调查后，我们决定受理你方索赔并赔偿有关的损失金额。

18. Without sufficient evidence to support, your claim is untenable.

你方的索赔缺乏足够的证据，因此根本站不住脚。

19. They express that they are not in a position to entertain our claim.

他们表示不能接受我们的索赔要求。

Exercises

I Complete the following dialogues.

1. **A:** _____.
   （上次你们的货物中有两箱品质和规格与样品不符。）

   B: I don't know what is happening. There haven't been such things with us. Maybe the factory sent the wrong boxes.

2. **A:** Here is what differs from your sample.

   B: _____.
   （这样，我马上和厂方联系。）

3. **A:** _____.
   （这次是第一次出现的问题，所以我们不再深究了。）

   B: There won't be such things.

4. **A:** Well, do you remember the flour under Contract No. 397?

   B: _____?
   （记得，这批货到达你方港口了吗？）

5. **A:** _____.
   （根据鉴定证明书，有些货物遭到了严重损坏。）

   B: How is the damage?

II Situational practice.

Make dialogues according to the following situations.

1. Imagine you have found there is something wrong with your import products: the breakage of the packing. What kind of strategy will you take to complain and ask for a claim?

2. Your business partner Mr. Johnson asks for a claim to you, but you think it is unreasonable. And then how do you deal with your negotiation with Mr. Johnson about the claim.

对话汉译

▶ 对话 1   投诉货物质量

拜伦先生（B）向冯女士（F）投诉货物短重以及质量低劣问题，并要求索赔。

B: 冯女士，早上好。我是一家澳大利亚进出口公司的杰克·拜伦。

F: 早上好，拜伦先生。您有什么事吗？

B: 冯女士，我要跟您谈一件很不愉快的事情。

F: 您请讲。

B: 你方运来的货物与合同的规格不相符，这使我们亏了很多钱，所以我们认为你方应负责解决问题，并补偿我方的损失。

F: 别着急，我们真诚地欢迎对我们货物的任何批评。我们先来谈谈问题吧。

B: 货物一到，我们就进行了检查，令我们失望的是，我们发现货物短重。

F: 是吗？好的，我会查清楚货物为什么会重量不足。

B: 好吧！还有，我们觉得劣质货物比例太高。

F: 很抱歉您有这种感觉。众所周知，我们的产品在国际上享有盛誉。对我们质量的投诉真的非常少。不过，我保证，一定会认真调查这些问题，看看是不是我们的错误。

B: 好的，我会等您的调查结果。

（几天后）

F: 下午好，拜伦先生。我是冯赢。

B: 冯女士，下午好。很高兴您能来电。您找出问题的原因了吗？

F: 找到了。关于重量不足的原因，我得指出货物在装运前是过了磅的。货物单据证实了我们发货时，货物足重。我认为重量不足是在运输过程中发生的。因此，我认为你们应当向保险公司提出索赔，因为责任在他们身上。

B: 那么，质量低劣又是怎么回事呢？

F: 经过调查后，我们发现是在工厂里出的错。一些工人在包装时错将 103 号货品当成了 102 号。这两种型号是不同等级的产品。我们真的很抱歉，愿意接受你们的索赔。请告诉我们你们想要我们怎么做。

B: 你们可以更换所有的劣质产品，并赔偿我们的生意损失。

F: 可以！明天我们会派人到贵公司，就换货和赔偿一事进行洽谈。

B: 我非常欣赏你们在这件事情上采取的正确态度。真心地希望我们以后的业务往来能诸事顺利。

F: 请相信我，这只是个别情况。我肯定今后的业务往来会一帆风顺。

▶ 对话 2　就索赔细节进行磋商

朱先生（Z）和凯德女士（C）在就索赔细节进行商讨。

Z: 很高兴您能来，凯德女士。

C: 朱先生，很高兴见到您。我来这里是要调查一下贵方对包装破损提出的索赔一事。

Z: 由于我们已经给你方发了索赔通知，你们肯定已经知道我方索赔的细节。

C: 你们说有近 25% 的包装已经破损。

Z: 是的，我方认为这是由于不恰当的包装所致。

C: 我不这样认为。在我来这里之前，我对这批货的情况进行了检查，在记录里没有发现任何包装问题。我认为破损是由于野蛮装卸所致。因此，我建议你们向船运公司提出索赔。您知道这批货是以离岸价格成交的……

Z: 抱歉打断您一下，按照合同，不可以使用旧麻袋进行包装。遗憾的是，你用了 280 个旧麻袋。粗劣的包装才是破损的真正原因所在。如果你们不折不扣地执行合同，就不会发生任何破损。我们为什么要向船运公司索赔呢？又如何能期望他们受理我们的索赔呢？

C: 您说什么？您肯定上次的货物包装用了旧麻袋？

Z: 千真万确。这是中国商品检验局的检查报告，您可以看看。

C:（看过检验报告之后）我可以看一下货物吗？

Z: 当然可以。货物还在码头的仓库里，我们在等待你方的检查，走吧。

C:（在看完仓库的破裂包装后）我很想知道怎么会发生这种事情？我真无法忍受这种让人尴尬的错误，对此我深表歉意。

Z: 好了，不过重新包装的确花了我们很长时间，费用合计 5 000 元人民币。我们希望你们赔偿这笔费用及检查费。希望你们能认真地考虑我们的索赔。

C: 当然，我们理应按照合同办理。

Z: 听到您这样说我很高兴。谢谢您的合作。

▶ **对话 3** 就赔付比例进行磋商

何小姐（H）和詹姆斯先生（J）正在商谈赔付比例问题。

H: 詹姆斯先生，如果情况不那么严重，我不会亲自来这儿。你方提供的是倒签提单，我希望你方做出合理的解释。

J: 对所发生的事情我很抱歉。这批货耽搁了几周，我们无奈使用了倒签提单。

H: 在我们国家这样的事件极为严重。

J: 我来解释一下，合同规定的装运期是 5 月 8 日。但是，轮船在 5 月 8 日才到达港口。我们不可能在同一天完成装货再使船离港。

H: 不管什么原因，这笔交易是以到岸价为条件成交的。你们这些年一直在做出口生意，因此你们知道谁应该对装运发货负责。

J: 对不起，我们没想到给你方带来这么大的麻烦。

H: 这是违反商业惯例和相关法律的事情。你方应该做出相应的赔偿。

J: 那你有什么要求？

H: 赔偿 20%，没有商量的余地。

J: 那就意味着我方要掏出 35 000 美元，但无论如何我们都会接受的。

> **对话 4** 讨论脱水发霉蔬菜的责任及赔偿问题

赵女士（Z）和史密斯先生（S）在讨论谁该对脱水蔬菜的发霉负责，并对此进行赔偿。

Z: 史密斯先生，我想和你谈谈关于 100 箱脱水蔬菜的质量问题。两周前到的货，我们当即进行了检查。令我们吃惊的是，大约 10%的脱水蔬菜已发霉。这样的货物我们是不能接受的。

S: 有这么回事？我们还从未收到过这样的投诉呢。您有什么证据吗？

Z: 当然有。这是伦敦一家著名的实验室的检验报告。

S: 它牵涉到很多因素。况且，贵方检验员并没有提及造成损坏的原因。

Z: 检验员的报告中说，检验时货物的外包装都是完好无损的。所以很明显，造成损坏的原因是蔬菜在包装前没有彻底干透。

S: 如您所知，这批货在装船前有商品检验局检验过。他们的结论是，此货已很好地除去了水分，且达到了出口的标准。

Z: 我想贵方检验局进行检验时，只随机地挑了几包，而这几包恰巧达到了标准。由于问题蔬菜的数量只是整批货物的 10%，我想贵方应该赔偿我们损失才算合理。

S: 我们事前已有协议，任意抽取这批货物的 10%进行检验，其检验证明是不可更改的且对双方都有约束力。我们认为，你们应该向保险公司索赔，因为损失发生在装船后。

Z: 我们已经联系过保险公司，但他们拒绝承担任何责任。他们将此事故归咎于长途海运中受潮的结果。

Extended Reading

Making A Claim

When making a claim, the buyer must prove that it is the seller's responsibility for the damage or loss of the goods. If he indeed can prove this, the seller is obligated to compensate the buyer. This is where the inspection certificate and B/L come in. The inspection certificate states the condition of the goods before loading. The B/L, as we know, is signed by an official of the shipping company when the goods have been loaded into the ship. He notes on the B/L that the consignment is "on board" and whether it is in "good order and condition" or not. So, both of these documents are used as evidence of the condition and/or weight of the goods when making a claim. Of course, the conflict appears when the goods are found to be damaged or of short weight when reaching the destination. You will then have an inspection certificate, which is not in agreement with the first certificate and/or the B/L. This is when the buyer presents his claim accompanied by inspection certificates to the seller for compensation. For instance, if a cargo of volcanic rocks arrives at a port, let's say, San Francisco, and it's found to be 20 tons short of the agreed weight, the buyer would take his claim with the appropriate documents to the seller. If he can prove that the seller was negligent in supplying the proper quantity or that the loss occurred at a time when the seller was still responsible for the consignment, such as, during shipping on a CIF basis, then the seller would most likely seek to find a way to satisfy his customer. Short weight is one of many possible claims. All of which would have a similar process: proving the occurrence of a discrepancy in the consignment and then proving whose responsibility it comes under.

Topic discussion:

1. What must the buyer do if he is going to making a claim?
2. What is used as evidence when making a claim?

 其他常用词汇和短语

供货不及时：

compensation   *n.* 补偿

delay   *v.* & *n.* 耽搁，延误

dispatch   *v.* & *n.* 发送

have no way out   没有别的办法

hinder   *v.* 阻止，阻碍

obligation   *n.* 义务，责任

vessel had run a ground   船只搁浅

错发货物：

awful   *a.* 糟糕的

coincide with   与……相符

critical   *a.* 批评的，挑剔的

lodge a claim   提出索赔

merchandise   *n.* 商品，货物

regrettable   *a.* 可叹的，可惜的，
          抱歉的

substitute   *v.* 代替

understandable   *a.* 体谅的

质量投诉：

convincing *a.* 有说服力的

corrode *v.* 腐蚀，侵蚀，锈蚀

defect *n.* 缺陷，缺点，瑕疵

promptly *ad.* 立刻地，立即地

reliable *a.* 可靠的

terminate *v.* 终结，终止

wharf *n.* 码头

短重投诉：

allowance *n.* 宽容，溢短重限度

amicably *ad.* 友好地，友善地

business deal 商务交易

Commodity Inspection and Quarantine
　　Bureau 商品检验检疫局

evaporation *n.* 蒸发

in transit 在途中

intact *a.* 完整的，未损坏的

货物损坏：

half price 半价

maritime accident 海上事故

surveyor's report 鉴定证明书

warrant *v.* 保证

要求退货：

cargo *n.* 货物

confirm *v.* 证实，确认

reveal *v.* 显示，揭示

接受索赔：

look into 调查

representative *n.* 代表

拒绝索赔：

deteriorated *a.* 变坏的

due to 由于

inherent vice 本身性质

legibly *ad.* 清楚地

make up to 补偿

moisture *n.* 潮气

qualification *n.* 限制，保留

stink *n.* 臭味

诉诸仲裁：

conciliation *n.* 调解	plaintiff *n.* 原告
council *n.* 委员会	proof *n.* 证据
customary practice *n.* 惯例	the defendant 被告
enforce *v.* 强制执行	

Appendix A   Glossary
词 汇 表

Words
单   词

acceptable   *a.* 可以接受的，可以使用的

adopt (employ, use)   *v.* 采用（某种价格术语）

advance   *v.* 提前

agent   *n.* 代理，代办处

aisle   *n.* 观众人行过道或通道

allowance   *n.* 宽容，溢短重限度

amends   *n.* 赔偿，赎罪

amicably   *ad.* 友好地，友善地

antedate   *v.* 把……上的日期填早（若干时间）

appearance   *n.* 外观，外表

arbitration   *n.* 仲裁

assembly   *v.* 展位搭建

assent   *n.* 同意，赞成

assurance   *n.* 有把握，放心

assure   *v.* 向……保证

attendance   *n.* 展览会人数

attendee   *n.* 展览会的参加者

attributable   *a.* 可归因于……的，由……引起的

awful   *a.* 糟糕的

background   *n.* 底色

balance   *n.* 余款，余额

bargain   *v.* 讨价还价

bid   *n. & v.* 递价，出价，递盘（由买方发出）

bindng   *a.* 有约束力的，附有义务的

blueprint   *n.* 展位设计施工图

booth   *n.* （隔开的）小房间，封闭的隔间，展示间，货摊，展位

breakage   *n.* 破坏，毁损，断裂

bureau   *n.* 局，处，所

calamity   *n.* 灾难，灾害

candidly   *ad.* 坦诚地，率直地，直率而诚恳地

capacity   *n.* 容量

cardboard   *n.* 硬纸板

cargo   *n.* 货物

carnet   *n.* 允许展品临时出口的海关批准文件

cartage   *n.* 货物运输费（或指展品从港口到展馆的短距离运输）

collision   *n.* 碰撞

commencement   *n.* 开始，开端

commit   *v.* 使承担任务

commitments   *n.* 所承诺的事

compel   *v.* 强迫，不得不

compensate　*v.*　赔偿

compensation　*n.*　补偿

competitive　*a.*　竞争的，有竞争性的

complicated　*a.*　复杂的

component　*n.*　组成部分

comprehensively　*ad.*　全面地，彻底地

concession　*n.*　让步，迁就，让与

conciliation　*n.*　调解

conclude　*v.*　结束，议定

concrete　*a.*　具体的，有形的

confidential　*a.*　保密的

configuration　*n.*　配置

confirm　*v.*　证实，确认

confirmation　*n.*　确认

conformity　*n.*　相似，符合，适合，一致

consignee　*n.*　（展品）收货人

consignment　*n.*　交付，委托

contingent　*n.*　偶然，意外

convention　*n.*　大型会议、展览或者两者兼而有之

convincing　*a.*　有说服力的

cooperation　*n.*　合作

corrode　*v.*　腐蚀，侵蚀，锈蚀

council　*n.*　委员会

countermand　*v.*　改变（订货），取消（订货），撤回

counter-offer　*n.*　还盘

critical　*a.*　批评的，挑剔的

customary practice　*n.*　惯例

customs　*n.*　海关

dampness　*n.*　受潮，潮湿

dealer (distributor)　*n.*　经销商

decline　*v.*　下降，下跌

defect　*a.*　缺陷，缺点，瑕疵

dehydrate　*v.*　脱水，失水

delay　*v. & n.*　耽搁，延误

delivery　*n.*　交货

design　*n.*　款式

desirable　*a.*　称心如意的

deteriorated　*a.*　变坏的

devastating　*a.*　毁灭性的

device　*n.*　手段，手法，技巧，设备

discrepency　*n.*　差异

discrete　*a.*　分离的，分立的

dishonor　*v.*　拒付

dismantle　*v.*　撤展

dispatch　*v. & n.*　发送

display　*n.*　展示，展览，陈列

dispute　*n.*　纠纷，争执

disqualification　*n.*　不合格

distinctive　*a.*　独特的

distraction　*n.*　分散注意力（或分心）的事物

dock　*n.*　码头

double-decker　*n.*　双层展位（摊位）

drawback　*n.*　退税

drayage　*n.*　货运（专指把展品从码头运到展馆摊位及在展览会结束后把储存的空箱运到展台，并把回运展品再运到码头的运输业务）

duress　*n.*　强迫，威胁

duty　*n.*　关税

economically　*ad.*　经济地，便宜地

effective　*a.*　有效的

employ　*v.*　用……计价，采用……

enforce　*v.*　强制执行

enhance　*v.*　提高，增强

entertain　*v.*　准备考虑

entity　*n.*　实体

equitable　*a.*　公平的，公正的，合理的

evaporation　*n.*　蒸发

excuse　*n.*　借口，理由

explosion　*n.*　爆炸

exquisite　*a.*　优美的，高雅的，精巧的，精致的

extrinsic　*a.*　外在的，非本质的

facilitate　*v.*　使更容易，便于，促进

facility　*n.*　便利

favor　*v.*　有利于

favorable　*a.*　优惠的

finish　*n.*　（家具等表面的）罩面

fragile　*a.*　易碎的，易损坏的

freight　*n.*　货运，运费

freighter　*n.*　承运人，货船

frequent　*a.*　时常发生的

fruition　*n.*　成就，实现

gathering　*n.*　集会，聚会

handling　*n.*　装卸，操纵

hedge　*v.*　规避，避免

hinder　*v.*　阻止，阻碍

hookup　*n.*　连接线路

hover　*v.*　徘徊于……，盘旋于……

identify　*v.*　识别，确定

illustration　*n.*　插图，说明，图解

incur　*v.*　招致，遭受

indemnify　*v.*　补偿，赔偿

indispensable　*a.*　必不可少的，必需的

inquirer　*n.*　询价者

inquiry　*n.*　询盘，询价

inspection　*n.*　检验

installment　*n.*　分期付款

insurance　*n.*　保险

insurer　*n.*　保险人，承保人

intact　*a.*　完整的，未损坏的

intantaneously　*ad.*　瞬间地，即刻地

interval　*n.*　（时间的）间隔

involve　*n.*　牵涉，包含

irrevocable　*a.*　不能取消的，不能撤回的

legibly　*ad.*　清楚地

liability　*n.*　责任

literature　*n.*　［总称］（商品说明书之类的）印刷品

lodge　*v.*　提出（报告、抗议、申诉等），正式提出

logistics　*n.*　物流

logo　*n.*　标识，商标

long-standing　*a.*　长期的

lorry　*n.*　运货汽车，卡车

mahogany　*n.*　红木

margin　*n.*　利润边际

marine　*a.*　海的，海上的，海事的，海运的

massage　*n./v.*　按摩，推拿

merchandise　*n.*　商品，货物

microwave　*n.*　微波炉

minus　*a.*　零下的

moderately　*ad.*　适当地，合适地，适度地

moisture　*n.*　潮气

moldy　*a.*　发霉的

non-negotiable　*a.*　不能议付的，非流通的

novel　*a.*　新颖的，新奇的

obligation　*n.*　义务，责任

offer　*n.& v.*　报盘

offeree　*n.*　被发价人，受盘人

offerer　*n.*　发价人，报盘人

offering　*n.*　奉献，提供，待售物

offeror　*n.*　发价（盘）人

offset　*v.*　弥补，抵消

optimize　*v.*　持乐观态度

origin　*n.* 原产地

original　*n.* 原件

overhead　*n.* 经常费用，开销

padauk　*n.* 紫檀

panel　*n.* 镶板，嵌板，护墙板

pay　*v.* 付款，支付，偿还

performance　*n.* 性能，表现

plaintiff　*n.* 原告

policy　*n.* 保险单

policyholder　*n.* 被保险人

premium　*n.* 保险费

prerequisite　*n.* 先决条件，前提，必备条件

prestige　*n.* 声誉，声望，威望，威信

price　*n.* 价格，定价，开价

priced　*a.* 已标价的，有定价的

pricing　*n.* 定价，标价

promote　*v.* 宣传，推销

prompt　*a.* 立刻的，迅速的

promptly　*ad.* 立刻地，立即地

proof　*n.* 证据

propagate　*v.* 传播，宣传

prospect　*n.* 前景，可能性，机会，可能成为主顾的人

prospective　*a.* 预期的，未来的，即将发生的

punctual　*a.* 准时的

qualification　*n.* 限制，保留

quotation　*n.* 报价

reasonable　*a.* 合理的

receipt　*n.* 收到，收讫

recognizable　*a.* 可辨认的，可认出的

recommend　*v.* 推荐

refusal　*n.* 拒绝

register　*v.* 登记，注册

regrettable　*a.* 可叹的，可惜的，抱歉的

release　*v. & n.* 释放，放行

reliable　*a.* 可靠的

representative　*n.* 代表

reserved　*a.* 有保留的，有条件的

responsibility　*n.* 责任

reveal　*v.* 显示，揭示

rock-bottom　*a.* 最低的

sailing　*n.* 航行，开船

scope　*n.* 范围

seaworthy　*a.* 适于航海的，经得起风浪的

shortly　*ad.* 立即，马上

shortweight　*n.* 短重

singular　*a.* 唯一的，独一的，单独的，罕见的，异常的

sinking　*n.* 沉没

specifications　*n.* 规范，规格

spoil　*v.* 损坏

stand　*v.* 经受得住

steamer　*n.* 轮船

stimulate　*v.* 激励，鼓励

stink　*n.* 臭味

stipulate　*v.* 约定，订立，规定，订明

strand　*v.* 使（船等）触礁，使搁浅

stranding　*n.* 搁浅

strengthen　*v.* 加固，使牢固

submit　*v.* 提交，提出

substitute　*v.* 代替

telex　*v.* 发用户电报

　　n. 用户电报

terminate　*v.* 终结，终止

termination　*n.* 终点，终止，结束

timely　*a.* 及时的

trademark　*n.* 商标

transaction　*n.*　交易

transit　*n.*　运输

transparent　*a.*　透明的

transship　*v.*　转船运输

turnover　*n.*　周转量，周转额

understandable　*a.*　体谅的

undertake　*v.*　承担，从事

underwriter　*n.*　保险，（特指）水险商

undue　*a.*　不适当的，不正当的

uphold　*v.*　维护，支持

utmost　*n.*　极限，竭尽所能

vessel　*n.*　船

warehouse　*n.*　仓库，货栈

warrant　*v.*　保证

wharf　*n.*　码头

wrapper　*n.*　包装物

Expressions
短　　语

7-piece set　7件一套，7件套

a series of　一系列

actual total loss　实际全损

adjustable standard　一种可以在其上随意安装展板的展架立杆

advance shipment　提前装运

air transportation insurance　航空运输保险

air freight　空运货物

airway bill/air bill　（货物）空运单

aisle signs　悬挂于展厅内用于标注过道名称或编号的过道标识

all risks　综合险，一切险

amended order　修改后的订单

an occasional inquiry　偶尔询盘

arrange/cover/effect/provide/take out insurance　投保，洽办保险

attendee brochure　（发送给参观商或观众以吸引他们赴展览会参观的）参观商手册

audio inquiry　声频询问，声音回答，声音询问

average price　平均价格

back order　积压的订单，到期尚未执行的订单

back-wall booth　靠墙展位，边缘展位

banking credit　银行信用

banner stand　易拉宝

bar code　条形码

base price　底价

be based upon　以……为基础，以……为条件

be equivalent to　相当于

be outbidding　高于……的价

bear inquiry　经得起追问

bedrock price　最低价

bill of lading (B/L)　装货凭单，提（货）单

bonded warehouse　保税仓库

bone yard　运输代理公司在展览现场所拥有或租用的用于存放展品空箱的仓库

booth area　摊位面积

booth number　摊位号

booth personnel　展台工作人员

booth sign　摊位楣板（用于标识参展商的名称、摊位号等）

booth size　展位尺寸

branch office　分支机构，分公司

business booth　洽谈室

business deal　商务交易

business scope　经营范围，业务范围

buying price　买价

buying team　（公司）采购小组

cable an offer/to telegraph an offer　电报（进行）报价

cash against aocuments（CAD）　凭单付现

cash on delivery（COD）　交货付现

cash with order（CWO）　随订单付现

cash in advance（CIA）　预付

cash with order（CWO）　预订金

catch the eye　引人注目

ceiling price　最高价，顶价

certificate of quality　质量证明书

certificate of weight　重量证明书

certificate of inspection　发运前对易变质物品等货物进行全面检查并证明其完好无损的证明文件

certificate of insurance　保险凭证

certificate of origin　原产地证明

CIF ex ship's hold　CIF 舱底交货价

CIF liner terms　CIF 班轮条件

clashing and breakage risk　碰损、破碎险

clean payment　单纯支付

closing price　收盘价

coincide with　与……相符

combined offer　联盘，搭配报盘

commercial credit　商业信用

commercial invoice　卖方发票，商业发票

Commodity Inspection and Quarantine Bureau　商品检验检疫局

concentration of offers　集中报盘

confirm one's order　确认订单

constructive total loss　推定全损

consumer show　面向公众开放的展览会，公共展

cooperative partner　合作伙伴

corner booth　位于两个或两个以上人行通道交汇处的展位

cost and freight（C&F）　成本加运费价，离岸加运费价

cost level　成本费用水平

cost of production　生产费用

cost price　成本价

cost, insurance and freight（CIF）　成本加保险费、运费价，到岸价

credit information　信用信息

credit inquiry　商业信用调查

credit inquiry division　信用咨询组

current price　时价，现价

declared value　申报价格

deferred payment　延期付款

delicate goods　易损易碎的货物

design of statistical inquiry　统计调查设计

direct fee　直接费用

dispatch money and demurrage　速遣费与滞期费

display case　展示柜

display rules and regulations　展览会规则

dock receipt　码头收货单据

double-faced panel　双面展板

down payment　预付定金，首付款

drayage contractor　货运服务商

drayage form　货运申请表

due to　由于

enter into　签订，缔约

entertain an offer　考虑报盘

European main ports　欧洲主要港口

ex dock duty paid　目的港码头完税交货价

ex dock duty unpaid　目的港码头未完税
　交货价

ex factory　工厂交货价

ex plantation　农场交货价

ex ship　目的港船上交货价

ex warehouse　仓库交货价

exceptional price　特价

exchange rate　汇率

execute an order　执行订单

expedite shipment　加速装运

extend an offer　延长报盘

extend shipment　延期装运

extra price　附加价

extraneous risks　附加险

fall in love with　开始喜欢某物

fall in with　与……巧合，与……相称

finalize a transaction　达成交易

firm offer　实盘

firm price　实价，实盘

floor plan　会场平面图

FOB liner terms　FOB 班轮条件

FOB plane　飞机离岸价（用于紧急情况）

FOB stowed　船上交货并理舱价

FOB trimmed　船上交货并平舱价

FOB under tackle　FOB 吊钩下交货价

for our file　供我方存档

force majeure　不可抗力

forward an offer/to send an offer　寄送报盘

free alongside ship (FAS)　船边交货价

free from particular average (FPA)　平安险

free on board (FOB)　船上交货价，离岸价

free on rail (FOR)　火车交货价

free on truck (FOT)　汽车交货价

freight cost　运输成本

freight forwarder　运输公司，转运公司

freight paid in advance　预付运费

fresh or rainwater damage　淡水雨淋险

general average (GA)　共同海损

get a bid　得到递价

get an offer/to obtain an offer　获得……报盘

give an offer　给……报盘

going price　现价

gross price　毛价

gross weight　毛重

gunny bags　黄麻袋

half price　半价

have in mind　意欲，打算

have no way out　没有别的办法

hold an inquiry into　对……进行调查

in accordance with　依照，按照

in sb's favor　以……为受益人

in stock　有库存

in strict confidence　严格保密

in transit　在途中

in written form　用书面形式

indicative mark　指示性标志

inherent vice　本身性质

initial order　首次订购，初订单

inquire about　对……询价

inquiry office　问询处

inquiry sheet　询价单

Institue Cargo Clauses (ICC)　（伦敦保险
　协会的）协会货物保险条款

insurance amount　保险额

insurance certificate 保险凭证

insurance coverage 保险范围

insurance policy 保险单，投保单

insurance rate 保险费率

international inter-modal/multimodal/ combined transport 国际联运

keep inquiry in mind 记住询盘

leakage risk 渗漏险

legal capacity 法律能力

liner transport 班轮运输

lodge a claim 提出索赔

look into 调查

lump offer 综合报盘（针对两种以上商品）

make a bid 递价

make a deal 达成交易

make an offer for 对……报盘

make delivery 交货

make it a deal 成交

make prompt delivery 即期交货

make signature 签字

make up to 补偿

make/effect shipment 装运

margin of profit 边际利润，利润限度

marine insurance 海运险

marine perils and losses 海上风险与损失

marine policy 海运保险单

maritime accident 海上事故

market price 市价

maximum price 最高价

medium-sized computer 中型计算机

meet half way 各让一半

meet one's commitment 履行义务

meet one's requirement 满足要求

member of the trade 行业会员

metal strap 金属带

minimum price 最低价

mode of transport 运输方式

moderate price 公平价格

more or less 或多或少，大约，……左右

natural calamities 自然灾害

net price 净价

net weight 净重

new price 新价

nominal price 有行无市的价格

non-firm offer 虚盘

non-negotiable 不能议付的，非流通的

notice of readiness (N/R) 装卸准备就绪通知书

ocean freight 海运运费

ocean marine cargo insurance 海运货物保险

offer and acceptance by post 通过邮政报价及接受

offer for 对……报盘（报价）

offer letter 报价书

offer list/book 报价单

offer price 售价

offer sheet 出售货物单

offer subject to export/import license 以获得出口（进口）许可证为准的报盘

offer subject to first available steamer 以装第一艘轮船为准的报盘

offer subject to goods being unsold 以商品未售出为准的报盘

offer subject to our final confirmation 以我方最后确认为准的报盘

offer subject to our written acceptance

以我方书面接受为准的报盘

offer subject to prior sale 以提前售出为
准的报盘

offer subject to sample approval 以样品
确定后生效为准的报盘

offer subject to your reply reaching here
以你方答复到达我地为准的报盘

offering date 报价日

offering period 报价有效期限

official offer 正式报价（报盘）

old price 旧价

on inquiry 经调查，经询问

on the high side 偏高

opening price 开价，开盘价

optional port 选择性港口

order acceptance 订单确认书

order form 订购单

original price 原价

overland insurance 陆上险

parcel post insurance 邮包险

partial delivery 分批交货，分批装运

partial shipment 分批装运

pass over 转给，转嫁

pay on delivery（POD） 货到付款

pay order 支付凭证

pay... Co. or order (pay to the order of...
Co.) 付……公司或其指定人

pay… Co. not negotiable 付……公司，
不准疏通

pay… Co. only 仅付……公司

payment agreement 支付协定

payment at maturity 到期付款

payment by banker 银行支付

payment by installment 分期付款

payment by remittance 汇拨支付

payment for（in）cash 现金支付，付现

payment in advance 预付（货款）

payment in full 全部付讫

payment in kind 实物支付

payment in part 部分付款

payment on terms 定期付款，按条件付款

payment order 付款通知

payment respite 延期付款

payment terms 付款方式，付款条件

place a trial order with 向……试购

plastic wares 塑料器具，塑料制品

port of destination 目的港

port of shipment 装运港

preferential offer 优先报盘

present price 现价

prevailing price 现价

price calculation 价格计算

price card 价格目录

price contract 价格合约

price control 价格控制

price current 市价表

price effect 价格效应

price format 价格目录，价格表

price index/price indices 物价指数

price limit 价格限制

price list 定价政策，价格目录，价格单

price of commodities 物价

price of factory 厂价

price per unit 单价

price ratio 比价

price regulation 价格调整

price structure 价格构成

price support 价格支持

price tag　价格标签，标价条

price terms　价格条款

price theory　价格理论

priced catalogue　定价目录

pricing cost　定价成本

pricing method　定价方法

pricing policy　定价政策

progressive payment　分期付款

promoting the sales　促销

purchase list　采购单

regular customer　老顾客，常客，老主顾

renew an offer/reinstate an offer　恢复报盘

repeat order　续订订单

rest assured　放心

rest assured that…　尽管放心……

retail price　零售价

risk to shortweight (shortweight risk)　短重险

rock-bottom price　最低价

ruling price　市价，时价

sales conditions　销售条件

sales confirmation　销售确认书

sales contract　销售合同

selling price　卖价

service fee　服务费

shipping by chartering　租船运输

shipping mark　唛头

shipping/shipment advice　装船通知

sign a treaty　签订条约

sign and return a copy of… for one's file　签退一份……以供某人存档

simple payment　单纯支付

something goes wrong　某事上出了问题，在某事上出现差错

sound and intact　完整无缺

special discount　特别折扣

special orders　特殊订货

special price　特价

specific inquiry　具体询盘

status inquiry　信用状况调查，资信调查

status report　资信报告

strikes, riot and civil commotion (SRCC)　罢工、暴动、民变险

subject to　以……为条件，以……为准

submit an offer　提交报盘

survey report　调查报告

surveyor's report　鉴定证明书

sweating and heating risks　受潮受热险

taint of odour risk　串味险

terms and conditions　交易条件

terms of payment　付款条件

the bank interest　银行利息

the defendant　被告

the preference of one's offer　优先报盘

the press　新闻界

the refusal of payment　拒付

theft, poilferage and non-delivery (TPND)　偷窃提货不着险

third party　第三方

time charter　定期租船

transshipment to be allowed　可以转船运输

treat as　作为……看待

trial order　试订单

trust form　委托表

usual terms　普通条件，正常条件

vessel had run a ground　船只搁浅

veterinary inspection certificate　动物检

疫证明

voyage charter 航次运输，程租船

war risk 兵险（战争险）

warning mark 警示标志

waterproof paper 防水纸

wholesale price 批发价

wild speculation 漫天要价

with particular average（WPA） 水渍险
（单独海损险）

work three shift 三班工作

References
参 考 文 献

[1] JU C A. 商务英语全能王[M]. 巨小卫，译. 西安：陕西师范大学出版社，2010.

[2] 陈祥国，袁秋红. 商务英语听说[M]. 北京：对外经济贸易大学出版社，2008.

[3] 高宝虹，孙晓丹. 商务英语口语通关[M]. 武汉：华中科技大学出版社，2002.

[4] 葛亚军. 商务英语口语[M]. 天津：天津科技翻译出版社，2005.

[5] 顾乾毅. 商务英语口语 900 句[M]. 广州：广东世界图书出版社，2004.

[6] 浩瀚. 商务英语情景会话模板[M]. 北京：国防工业出版社，2007.

[7] 李地. 商务英语会话[M]. 北京：中国经济出版社，2008.

[8] 廖清文，夏元生. 商贸实用英语会话[M]. 天津：天津大学出版社，2002.

[9] 廖瑛. 实用商务英语口语教程[M]. 武汉：华中科技大学出版社，2008.

[10] 刘文宇. 商务英语口语大全[M]. 大连：大连理工大学出版社，2007.

[11] 盛丹丹. 商务谈判高手过招[M]. 北京：国防工业出版社，2010.

[12] 孙耀远. 商务英语听说教练[M]. 大连：大连理工大学出版社，2007.

[13] 王乃彦. 商务英语口[M]. 北京：对外经济贸易大学出版社，2008.

[14] 王伟，周树玲. 商务英语 900 句[M]. 北京：对外经济贸易大学出版社，2008.

[15] 王艳. 全方位商务英语口语[M]. 北京：对外经济贸易大学出版社，2005.

[16] 王玉章，王怡. 商务英语会话[M]. 天津：天津大学出版社，2005.

[17] 翁风翔. 当代国际商务英语口语与口译[M]. 上海：上海交通大学出版社，2007.

[18] 辛欣. 商务英语脱口秀[M]. 北京：中国纺织出版社，2010.

[19] 朱立文，胡竟扬. 会展英语文萃选读[M]. 北京：中国海关出版社，2004.